The Lake Chelan Cookbook

A Culinary Journey Into the Lake Chelan Valley

Leo Montaigne

Elsewhere Publishing

An Elsewhere Publishing Book

Copyright 2024 by Leo Montaigne.

Printed in the United States of America.

lakechelancookbook.com

ISBN: 979-8-9864535-3-8

CONTENTS

THE LAKE CHELAN COOKBOOK

INTRODUCTION

Well, hello. Pull up a chair. Is that your stomach rumbling? When's the last time you ate, friend? If grub's what you're after, you've come to the right place. There's enough in this here book to put your hunger right out of its misery and then some.

Just what is this book, you say? It don't look like your average cookbook, now does it? No sir. If average is what you're hankering for, you're better off closing this particular volume, and we can part ways now before you part with your hard-earned dollars.

But if you've got a mind for something a little different, well...sit back and stay awhile. Let me tell you what you're holding in your hands here, cause it's something special.

This ain't your grandaddy's cookbook, as the saying goes. What you got here is a dive into the deep end of the culinary waters of Lake Chelan. We sat down with 19 restaurant owners and chefs from around the Valley. We interviewed all of them and requested recipes from those fine folks, and 32 recipes were delivered before we went to press. You'll find those recipes in these pages, and you'll find those interviews here as well.

But we didn't stop there. We got in touch with local residents who submitted dozens of recipes as well. Family recipes. Traditional recipes. Long-held secrets maybe. Who knows. But we got them.

And just because we don't like to leave stones unturned, we perused half a dozen Chelan cookbooks written over the decades. Collections put together by folks like the Lake Chelan Hospital, the PUD, the Women's Genealogical Society, and the like. You'll find recipes from those books updated, altered and refreshed in these pages under the label "Inspired By" along with their original authors.

Thus if you were to read this culinary roadmap from one end to the other, you would find yourself well educated on just where things stand here in the Valley, from a food and sustenance point of view anyway.

You'd learn about a family that moved here after their house was blown away by Katrina. You'd learn about a judge in a dry parish in Iowa who crossed the country by train, hopped off and walked 61 miles before finally finding himself a home here beside the lake. You'd even learn useless facts to wow your friends at parties, such as the fact that there are companies that make starch for cardboard boxes. To make them stiffer, of course.

And you just may learn to cook like someone who lives by the lake. Stranger things have happened.

Leastways, I'm glad you're here. We've barely gotten to know each other and I like you already. I got an eye for people. I know the good ones right off. And you, friend, you're a keeper.

So now that we're acquainted, don't let me take up no more of your time. There's grub to be had. And trust me, it's good stuff. I should know. I had to eat a lot of it to write this book.

As they say in other parts of the world: adios.

Leo Montaigne

YOU WILL FIND IT AT CHELAN

Reprinted From the *Chelan Leader, October 1910*

Chelan is located at the outlet of Lake Chelan, one of the largest and most attractive mountain lakes in the world, which reaches from a point within two and one-half miles of the Columbia River to the heart of the main range of the Cascades. The town is incorporated, and has a population of 800. It is the principal business point of a fruit growing, lumbering and mining territory 1,000 square miles in extent with a present population of 3,000 or more.

The town has: nine brick blocks, four churches, a large auditorium and other public and business buildings; one bank, one department store, two big general stores, two hardware stories, two drug stores, two hotels, one grocery and feed store, one exclusive shoe store, one clothing store, one jewelry store, meat market, blacksmith shop, barber shop, paint shop, bakery, restaurant, livery and transfer, steam laundry, saloon, billiard hall, and an extensive sawmill and planing mill plant, two dentists, two physicians, three attorneys and four real estate firms.

The churches are Methodist, Episcopalian, Catholic and Seventh Day Adventist. Fine large brick public school building, with seven departments: excellent educational facilities; eight teachers; high school accredited by state university and state board of education. A sanitarium with modern equipment; good hotel accommodations. Good society, the police court records showing but one arrest in two years.

Splendid electric light and water systems, with current light and power, and water for domestic use and irrigation at reasonable rates.

THE RECIPES

LOCAL RESTAURANTS

COMMUNITY RECIPES

LOCAL RESTAURANTS

Apple Cup

CAFE

Pumpkin Crisp

INGREDIENTS

- 1 Large Can Pumpkin
- 3 Eggs
- 1 Can Evaporated Milk
- 1 Cup Sugar
- 1/2 Teaspoon Salt
- 4 Teaspoons Pumpkin Pie Spice
- 1 Box Yellow Cake Mix
- 3/4 Cup Chopped Walnuts
- 1 Cup Melted Butter

DIRECTIONS

Beat first six ingredients together & pour into a 9 x 13 greased pan. Sprinkle yellow cake mix on top.

Sprinkle with walnuts. Pour melted butter over entire mixture.

Bake 30 minutes at 350 degrees. Then lower temp to 325 and bake for another 30 minutes.

Mixture should be set except for small area in the center which will set as it cools.

FROM THE INTERVIEW

Apple Cup

We originally opened in 1957. It was called the Snack Shack back then, but the name was changed. The Apple Cup was the name of the hydroplane races that were held here in Chelan from 1957 to 1960.

This was my family's restaurant. I was eight when my parents bought it. I've been running around here since I was eight years old.

5

see page 146 for full interview

Blueberry
HILLS

Blueberry Danish Waffles

BLUEBERRY HILLS

INGREDIENTS

- 2 Cups Milk
- 1 Package Dry Yeast
- 1/4 Cup Water
- 2 Tablespoons Sugar
- 1 Teaspoon Salt
- 3 Eggs
- 1/4 Cup Salad Oil
- 2 Cups Flour

INSTRUCTIONS

Scald 2 cups of milk. Cool to lukewarm in mixing bowl. Dissolve 1 package of dry yeast in 1/4 cup warm water. Add milk and mix.

Then add: sugar, salt, eggs and salad oil.

Stir well.

Add 2 cups of flour. Stir until blended. Let rise once. Stir down and refrigerate until ready to make pancakes.

Stir before baking in waffle iron. Bake in waffle iron until golden brown.

To serve: add whipped cream and generous amount of blueberry pie filling (see next page). Garnish with fresh blueberries.

Blueberry Hills

Blueberry Pie Filling

INGREDIENTS

- 4 Cups Blueberries
- 1 Cup Sugar
- 1/3 Cup Cornstarch
- 1/4 Cup Lemon Juice

DIRECTIONS

Mix berries, sugar, and lemon juice in a heavy saucepan. Bring to boil. Stir frequently.

Try not to drool.

Mix cornstarch with enough water to make a paste. Pour into the berry mixture. Stir constantly until thick.

Cool.

Uses:

- Pie Filling
- Danish Waffle Topping
- Mending Broken Hearts
- Restoring Faith in Humanity
- Dying Man's Last Meal

SERVINGS	TIME	DELICIOUSNESS
1 PIE	15 mins	10

FROM THE INTERVIEW

Blueberry Hills

We put them in the ground the first year. But there were very few blueberries. We had 13,000 plants. Second year they doubled in size but there weren't enough to pick. Then we opened the third year.

So we're waiting for those blueberries to ripen, and every day we'd go out to look. But they're not ready. And finally the day comes, we know they're ripe and tomorrow's gonna be the day we can pick these big beautiful blueberries.

And we go out there and they're gone. The birds had been waiting just like us, and the birds got every single one of them.

see page 151 for full interview

Broken
COMPASS

Broken Compass at Riverwalk Inn

Blueberry Scone

INGREDIENTS

DRY MIX
- 2 Cups All Purpose Flour
- 1/2 Cup Granulated Sugar
- 2 1/2 Teaspoons Baking Powder
- 1/2 Teaspoon Salt
- 1 Teaspoon Cinnamon

WET MIX
- 1 Large Egg
- 1/2 Cup Heavy Cream
- 2 Teaspoons Vanilla

PLUS
- 1 Stick Butter Cut Into 1 Centimeter Cubes
- Frozen Blueberries
- Turbinado Sugar

DIRECTIONS

Cut butter into cubes and place in freezer to cool while you prepare your mixes.

To prepare dry mix, combine all ingredients and stir with hands or whisk. Set aside.

In a small bowl, combine all wet ingredients and whisk. Set aside.

Add cold cubed butter to your dry mix. Combine until butter is evenly spread around the flour. Make a well in the middle and pour in wet mix.

With your hands, stir and mix the ingredients together. When the dough comes to a crumbly texture, add a heaping cup of frozen blueberries. Then mix/fold blueberries gently into the dough.

Pour dough out onto a baker's block or stainless steel counter. Press together until you get a flat disc shape about 1 inch thick and 6 inches wide. If dough is too dry and won't come together, wet with small amounts of heavy cream.

Cut dough into 6 even pie-shaped slices. Place on a baking sheet lined with baking paper. Sprinkle with Turbinado sugar.

Bake at 325 degrees for 10 to 15 minutes.

SERVINGS	TIME	DELICIOUSNESS
6	40 mins	10

FROM THE INTERVIEW

Broken Compass:
We sat down and thought: what would we eat? You know, what would we make for dinner? What would we want for lunch? We didn't really think about what other people would want necessarily. We started with ourselves. What would we want to eat for breakfast? And then we worked from there. Everything on the menu is something we've made at home ourselves. Nothing is a recipe we found online or anything like that. It's just food we've made and food we love.

see page 156 for full interview

Campbell's Pub and Veranda

Apple Oat Pancakes

INGREDIENTS

- 4 Cups Whole Wheat Flour
- 4 Cups All Purpose Flour
- 1 Cup Cornmeal
- 3 Tablespoons Baking Powder
- 2 Tablespoons Baking Soda
- 1/2 Tablespoon Salt
- 20 Ounces Quick Oats
- 2 Sticks Butter Cubed
- 1/4 Cup Honey
- 3 Whole Eggs
- 4 Cups Buttermilk
- 2 Granny Smith Apples (Diced)

DIRECTIONS

Combine flours, cornmeal, baking powder, baking soda, salt and oats. In a mixer, combine with cold cubed butter until incorporated.

Combine honey, eggs & buttermilk together in a large bowl and stir to incorporate. Combine your two mixtures together.

Preheat pan on medium heat. Add butter and melt until foaming subsides. Ladle batter into the center of the pan. Sprinkle with cubed apples on top. Cook until edges start to bubble and brown. Flip. Cook until bottom edges brown.

Remove pancakes and serve with butter and syrup.

SERVINGS	TIME	DELICIOUSNESS
I	20	IO
	mins	

CAMPBELL'S RESORT: A TIMELINE

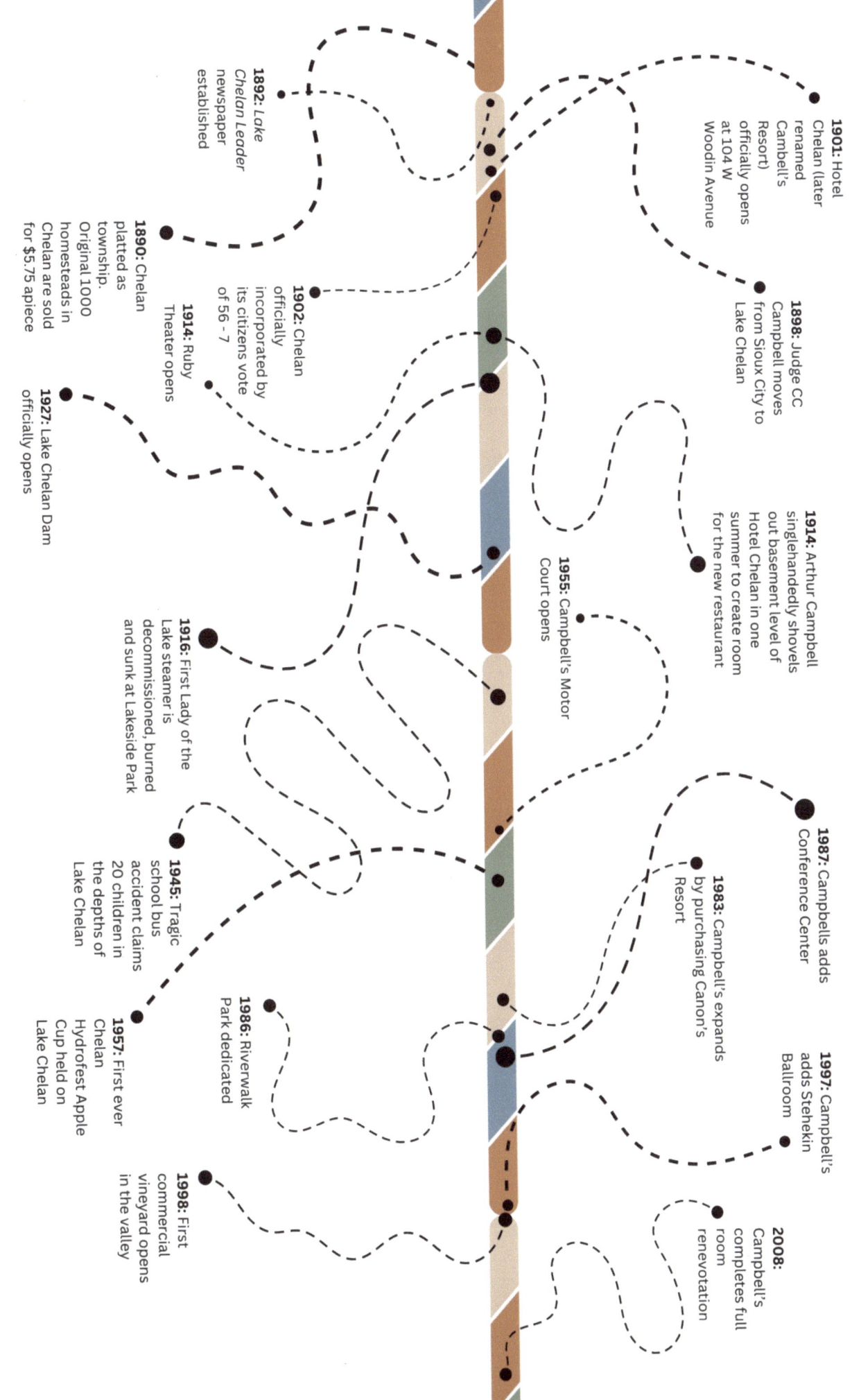

1890: Chelan platted as township. Original 1000 homesteads in Chelan are sold for $5.75 apiece

1892: *Lake Chelan Leader* newspaper established

1898: Judge CC Campbell moves from Sioux City to Lake Chelan

1901: Hotel Chelan (later renamed Campbell's Resort) officially opens at 104 W Woodin Avenue

1902: Chelan officially incorporated by its citizens vote of 56 - 7

1914: Ruby Theater opens

1914: Arthur Campbell singlehandedly shovels out basement level of Hotel Chelan in one summer to create room for the new restaurant

1916: First Lady of the Lake steamer is decommissioned, burned and sunk at Lakeside Park

1927: Lake Chelan Dam officially opens

1945: Tragic school bus accident claims 20 children in the depths of Lake Chelan

1955: Campbell's Motor Court opens

1957: First ever Chelan Hydrofest Apple Cup held on Lake Chelan

1983: Campbell's expands by purchasing Canon's Resort

1986: Riverwalk Park dedicated

1987: Campbells adds Conference Center

1997: Campbell's adds Stehekin Ballroom

1998: First commercial vineyard opens in the valley

2008: Campbell's completes full room renovation

Campbell's Pub and Veranda

Fire Pasta

INGREDIENTS

- 1 Chicken Breast (or 2 Boneless Skinless Chicken Thighs)
- Kosher Salt
- Fresh Ground Pepper
- 2 Tablespoons Vegetable Oil
- 2 Tablespoons Worcestershire
- 2 Tablespoons Frank's Original Hot Sauce
- Pinch of Chili Flake
- Heaping 1/2 Cup Heavy Cream
- Hotel Butter*
- 1/4 Cup Parmesan Cheese
- 7 Oz Fettuccine Pasta (Cooked)

DIRECTIONS

Cut chicken into 1 inch wide strips. Then warm a pan over medium heat. Add oil, salt, and pepper. Cook chicken in the pan until about 3/4 cooked.

Add Worcestershire and Frank's. Then add heavy cream and chili flakes.

Bring to a boil and add pasta to the pan. Reduce until noodles are hot and cream has a thick consistency but is not broken.

Fold in the Hotel Butter and serve in a pasta bowl. Generously sprinkle with parmesan cheese.

Optional: garnish with parsley and toasted garlic chips.

*Hotel Butter is butter, minced garlic, lemon juice and salt and pepper whipped together.

SERVINGS	TIME	DELICIOUSNESS
1	20 mins	10

Campbell's Pub and Veranda

Salmon Romesco

INGREDIENTS

- 4 King Salmon Filets (Skin On & Scored)
- 2 Cups Charred Cauliflower
- 3 Handfuls Wild Baby Arugula
- 3/4 Cup Pecan Romesco
- 2 Charred Lemons (Halved)
- Extra Virgin Olive Oil
- Salt & Pepper

DIRECTIONS

Preheat oven to 350 degrees.

Season salmon with salt & pepper generously on both sides. Preheat pan on medium-high heat. Add salmon skin side down. Cook about 1 minute (do not move in pan).

Move pan to preheated oven for 6 to 8 minutes.

On a warmed plate, pool Romesco sauce (see next page for recipe) on one side. Lay salmon next to sauce.

Serve with charred cauliflower.

Campbell's Pub and Veranda

Pecan Romesco Sauce

INGREDIENTS

- 2 Quarts Roasted Piquillo Peppers (Drained)
- 1 Cup Roasted Garlic Cloves
- 1/2 Cup Sherry Vinegar
- 1 Quart Toasted Pecans
- 3 Tablespoons Salt
- 2 Teaspoons Pepper
- 1 Pint Extra Virgin Olive Oil

DIRECTIONS

In blender or food processor, blend all ingredients (except olive oil) until smooth.

Stream in olive oil to emulsify.

Add additional vinegar, salt and pepper to taste.

Sauce is designed to pair with Salmon Romesco recipe.

SERVINGS
4

TIME
10
mins

DELICIOUSNESS
10

Campbell's Pub & Veranda

Rum Raisin Sauce

INGREDIENTS

- 2 Cups Brown Sugar
- 1 Cup Butter
- 3/4 Cups Milk
- Juice of 3 Lemons
- 1 Teaspoon Cinnamon
- 1 Cup Raisins
- 1/2 Cup Meyers Dark Rum

DIRECTIONS

Combine all ingredients in a saucepan. Bring to boil.

Remove from heat and let cool.

Drizzle over Apple Orchard Ice Cream (see previous recipe).

SERVINGS	TIME	DELICIOUSNESS
12	10 mins	10

Campbell's Pub & Veranda

Country Chicken

INGREDIENTS

- 4 Chicken Breasts
- 2 Cups Flour Dredge (Flour/Salt/Pepper)
- 2 Tablespoons Butter
- 2 Tablespoons Olive Oil
- 1/4 Cup Shallots
- 1 Large Apple w/Skin (Cored & Cut Into Wedges)
- 1/3 Cup Dry Sherry
- 1 Cup Chicken Stock
- 1/2 Cup Heavy Cream

DIRECTIONS

Flatten chicken in seasoned flour. Melt butter and oil on medium heat in large saucepan.

Add chicken and brown on both sides (do not cook all the way through). Remove and set aside.

Add shallots to the pan & stir for 2 minutes. Add apples, chicken stock & sherry. Bring to simmer and lower heat. Stir to remove brown bits from bottom of pan.

Return chicken to the pan. Turn chicken to cover with sauce. If sauce thickens too much, add more stock to thin. Turn heat to low.

Add cream. Stir to combine. Cook chicken until done.

Add salt & pepper to sauce to taste (ground nutmeg is an optional but pleasant addition as well).

Plate with sauce on top with apples and fresh chopped chives.

SERVINGS	TIME	DELICIOUSNESS
4	30 mins	10

Campbell's Pub & Veranda

Apple Orchard Ice Cream

INGREDIENTS

- 15 Apples
- 6 Cups Sugar
- 1 Cup Flour
- 1 1/2 Teaspoon Cinnamon
- 2 Cups Pecan Pieces
- 3 Gallons Softened Vanilla Ice Cream

DIRECTIONS

Pell and cut apples. In a pot, stir together apples, sugar, flour and cinnamon.

Cook apple mixture on medium-high heat. Stir so that mixture does not scorch. Bring to boil and cook three minutes.

Remove from heat and add pecan pieces. Let cool.

Fold apple mixture into softened ice cream. Freeze immediately for 24 hours.

Serve with Merry's Rum Raisin Sauce (see next page).

SERVINGS	TIME	DELICIOUSNESS
12	45 mins	10

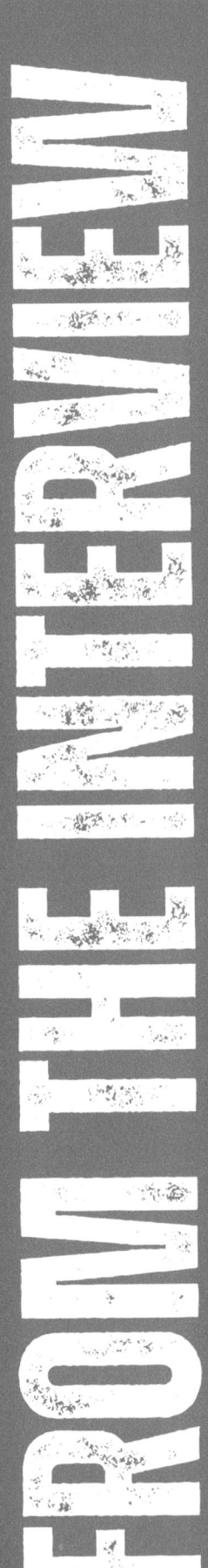

FROM THE INTERVIEW

february 2024

Tom Campbell

Our great, great grandfather, CC Campbell, came over from Sioux City in Iowa in the late 1800s. This was like the wild west out here. Cowboys, pioneers, stuff like that. He was a judge and a lawman in charge of a dry parish. No alcohol, right? He wasn't exactly the most popular guy around.

Eric Campbell

I think he may have honestly feared for his family's safety. So he made his way west. He went by himself at first from Sioux City. Hopped on a train and came out west.

Tom Campbell

He ended up in Wilbur, Washington. He walked from Wilbur to Chelan.

see page 160 for full interview

CJ's
GRILL

CJ's Grill

Jambalaya

INGREDIENTS

- 1 Pound Andouille Sausage (Sliced)
- 1 Pound Boneless Chicken Thighs
- 1 Cup Diced Onion
- 1 Cup Diced Bell Pepper
- 1 Cup Diced Celery
- 3 Cloves Minced Garlic
- 2 Cups Long Grain Rice
- 1 Can Diced Tomatoes
- 3 Cups Chicken Broth
- 2 Tablespoons Creole Seasoning
- 1 Teaspoon Dried Thyme
- 1 Teaspoon Paprika
- 1/4 Teaspoon Cayenne
- 2 Green Onions (Sliced)
- 1/4 Cup Chopped Parsley
- Salt & Pepper

DIRECTIONS

In Dutch oven, brown sausage until crispy. Remove and set aside. Add chicken to pot and cook until browned. Remove and set aside.

Add onions, bell peppers, celery and garlic and cook until softened. Stir in rice and cook until rice is lightly toasted. Add tomatoes, chicken broth, Creole, thyme, paprika and cayenne pepper. Season with salt & pepper to taste. Bring to boil.

Reduce heat, cover pot & simmer for 20 minutes or until rice is cooked through.

Stir in sausage and chicken and cook for an additional 5 minutes until meat is heated through.

Remove pot from heat and stir in green onions and parsley.

SERVINGS	TIME	DELICIOUSNESS
6	75 mins	10

CJ's Grill

Corn Maque Choux

INGREDIENTS

- 4 Ears Corn
- 4 Slices Bacon (Chopped)
- 1 Medium Yellow Onion (Chopped)
- 1 Red Bell Pepper (Chopped)
- 1 Jalapeno Pepper (Chopped)
- 1 Tablespoon Cajun Seasoning
- Salt & Pepper
- 1/4 Cup Chicken Stock
- 1/2 Cup Heavy Cream
- Hot Sauce

DIRECTIONS

Slice the corn kernels from cobs and set aside. Use dull edge of a knife to scrape the edges of the corn cob to release their "milk" into a bowl. Set aside.

Heat large pan to medium heat and add bacon. Cook until crispy. Stir in the corn, onion, peppers and Cajun. Add salt & pepper to taste. Cook until vegetables soften and begin to caramelize.

Add chicken stock and corn "milk" and simmer for 10 - 15 minutes. Mixture should thicken nicely.

Add heavy cream. Let warm for about two minutes and remove from heat.

SERVINGS	TIME	DELICIOUSNESS
6	75 mins	10

FROM THE INTERVIEW

CJ's Grill

Katrina was so huge. It took over three states: Alabama, Mississippi, Louisiana. The eye went right through Waverly where we lived. And those tight inner bands hit us hard.

We were two blocks from the beach. We ended up leaving. We discussed it a lot as a family whether we were going to leave or not. For years the storms had come and we had stayed. At first we thought, nah, we'll ride this one out. But eventually we changed our minds and we went to Georgia to wait.

On the way back, about five days after we left, we found bridges all washed out. We knew it was bad. And our house was just gone. Just gone. Whole house just blown away to Iowa or somewhere.

see page 168 for full interview

County
LINE

County Line

Smoked Mac & Cheese

INGREDIENTS

- 2 1/2 Cups Half & Half
- 6 Tablespoons Unsalted Butter
- 8 Oz Cream Cheese (Cubed)
- 1 Teaspoon Hot Sauce
- 1 Teaspoon Dry Mustard
- 3/4 Teaspoon Fresh Ground Black Pepper
- 3/4 Teaspoon Kosher Salt
- 1 1/2 Cup Shredded Cheddar Cheese
- 1 1/2 Cup Shredded Gouda Cheese
- 1 Cup Panko Breadcrumbs
- 16 Oz Dried Cavatappi Pasta

DIRECTIONS

Bring smoker to 180 degrees. In well-seasoned 12-inch cast-iron skillet, combine the following:

- Half and half
- 5 tablespoons butter
- Cream cheese
- Hot sauce
- Dry mustard
- Black pepper
- Salt
- Shredded cheese (cheddar & Gouda)

Bring a large pot of salted water to a boil. Add Cavatappi pasta. Cook for roughly 1 to 2 minutes *less* than stated on the package (you want the pasta a little underdone). Then drain pasta, rinse with cold water, and return to pot.

Remove sauce from heat and whisk until smooth. Pour the smoked sauce over the pasta. Stir to coat.

Increase smoker temperature to 350 degrees.

Clean the skillet. Grease with remaining butter. Pour macaroni & cheese into skillet. Place skillet into smoker and bake for 30 to 40 minutes.

Serve with breadcrumbs.

SERVINGS	TIME	DELICIOUSNESS
4	45 - 60 *mins*	10

Jalapeno Poppers

INGREDIENTS

- 8 Jalapeno Peppers
- Goat Cheese
- Bacon

DIRECTIONS

Preheat oven to 400 degrees.Cut Jalapeños in half longways. Leave stem on. Remove seeds. Fill with goat cheese.

Cut bacon in half longways. Wrap around Jalapeños.

Bake for about 15 minutes while your mouth waters.

Char Siu

INGREDIENTS

- 2 Pound Pork Tenderloin Cut Into 3x3 Inch Pieces
- 1/3 Cup Soy Sauce
- 3 Tablespoons Honey
- 3 Tablespoons Hoisin Sauce
- 3 Tablespoons Sugar
- 1/2 Teaspoon Chinese 5 Spice Powder
- 4 Garlic Cloves (Minced)
- 2 Tablespoons Fresh Ginger (Minced)
- 1 Tablespoon Red Food Coloring

DIRECTIONS

Set pork aside. Blend all other ingredients together to create marinade. Marinate the pork for 48 hours.

Preheat oven to 400 degrees.

Place a pan with about half an inch of water on the bottom rack of the oven.

Arrange the 3 inch pork chunks on a sheet pan with a wire rack. Place in the oven above the pan with the water in it. You should now have two items in the oven: the pan with the water and the sheet with the wire rack holding the pork.

Cook for 30 minutes. Rotate every 10 minutes until internal temperature reaches 160 to 165 degrees.

Place in refrigerator and serve cold with hot mustard, Hoisin & sesame seeds.

FROM THE INTERVIEW

Josh

With the food truck, everyone thinks you just roll up and start serving food. They don't think about how much prep there is, and also ensuring that the truck has fuel, that it has water. You have to have a drain for your gray water. On and on.

Allison

Or how hot it is in there. People never realize that.

Josh

You talk about heat. We have an AC unit, but it doesn't put out nearly enough cold air. There's a fryer in the truck running at 350 degrees. And the flat top at 400 degrees. Plus it's 100 degrees outside in the summer. That food truck is a sweat box. We had it up to 117 degrees inside there before.

see page 180 for full interview

Deb's
DELIGHTS

Deb's Delights

Chocolate Mousse

INGREDIENTS

- 10 Ounces Semi-Sweet Baking Chocolate (Chopped)
- 3 Large Eggs
- 1 Cup Heavy Whipping Cream

DIRECTIONS

Take out two eggs and separate yolks from whites. You will need both, so don't discard either.

Fill medium saucepan with inch of water and bring to boil. Place chocolate in a metal bowl large enough to put atop saucepan without touching the water. Set bowl into saucepan, simmer, and stir while chocolate melts.

In a large bowl, put 1 whole egg and 2 egg yolks and whisk. Set aside.

In a small bowl, whip 2 egg whites to stiff peaks.

Slowly whisk melted chocolate into egg yolk mixture. You don't want to scramble the eggs, so make sure chocolate is not hot. Mix well.

With rubber scraper, take 1/3 of whipped cream and fold into chocolate to loosen it up. Then take another 1/3 of whipped cream and fold it gently into chocolate.

Gently fold egg whites into chocolate. Don't beat out all the air. Fold in remaining whipped cream and egg whites until completely incorporated.

Place in serving bowl and chill for 2 hours.

SERVINGS	TIME	DELICIOUSNESS
6	30 mins	10

FROM THE INTERVIEW

Deb's Delights

Wedding cakes. I've been making wedding cakes for 26 years. I was working out of my home making cakes, three or four every summer. A friend of mine was a florist and she was doing a wedding with a bride who had very little money. She wanted to know if I'd make a cake for her. My friend knew I was pretty good with cakes.

That's really where it started, with wedding cakes. Later I became a pastry chef. And that led to opening my own place.

see page 188 for full interview

Goldie's
CAFE

Goldie's

Peacemaker Smoothie

INGREDIENTS

- 1/2 Cup Frozen Banana (Sliced)
- 1 Cup Frozen Strawberries
- 1/2 Cup Mango
- 12 Ounces Fresh Orange Juice

DIRECTIONS

Put all ingredients into a heavy duty blender (like a Vitamix) and blend until smooth.

If you don't have a heavy duty blender, you can still use a regular blender, but you should add more orange juice or reduce frozen fruit.

SERVINGS	TIME	DELICIOUSNESS
I	5 mins	IO

Golden Bowl

GOLDIE'S

INGREDIENTS

- 1 Cup Frozen Banana (Sliced)
- 1 Cup Frozen Strawberries
- 1/2 Pack of Acai
- 6 Ounces Unsweetened Almond Milk

TOPPING

- 1/4 Cup Granola
- 2 Fresh Strawberries
- Peanut Butter Drizzle
- Honey Drizzle
- Chocolate Chips

INSTRUCTIONS

Blend bananas, frozen strawberries, acai and almond milk in a heavy duty blender (like a Vitamix). If you don't have a heavy duty blender, add more liquid or reduce frozen fruit to make it easier to blend.

Scope blended mixture into a bowl and top with granola, fresh strawberries, drizzles and chocolate chips.

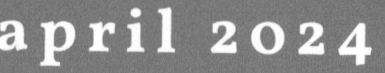

FROM THE INTERVIEW

april 2024

Goldie's

Moonpenny. It opened in July of 2020. And on the Goldie's side we couldn't have opened because we were still remodeling. We were adding walls, putting in the archway, adding bathrooms.

They're so different. I like to think of myself as a very creative person. I like each business for different reasons. I love food. I love clothes. It's great to be able to do both.

see page 192 for full interview

Lago
PASTA

Lago Pasta

Pomodoro Sauce

INGREDIENTS

- 1 Can San Marzano Tomatoes (2500g)
- 100 ml Extra Virgin Olive Oil
- 15 Grams Diced Shallots
- 2 Whole Garlic Cloves
- 1 Teaspoon Sicilian Dried Oregano
- 4 Fresh Basil Leaves
- 4 Grams Fine Sea Salt
- 2 Grams Fine Ground Black Pepper

DIRECTIONS

Crush tomatoes with hands or emulsion blender until the sauce is smooth with small chunks of tomato.

Saute shallot and garlic in olive oil over medium heat until shallots and garlic begin to turn gold. Stir regularly to avoid burning. Turn off heat and add oregano. Stir for 30 seconds.

Add crushed tomatoes and basil. Bring heat to medium high. Stir until sauce begins to simmer, making sure bottom does not burn. Turn heat to low, bringing sauce to low simmer and cook for 1 hour or until acidity is cooked out of the sauce.

Turn off heat.

Stir in salt and pepper.

Miles & Miles of Pasta

In peak season Lago Pasta produces roughly 200 pounds of pasta every day. To get a sense of how much pasta that is, we imagined 200 pounds of spaghetti noodles made each day of the summer and how far that would stretch if each noodle was put end to end.

1 POUND OF SPAGHETTI IS ROUGHLY 500 NOODLES. EACH NOODLE IS 12 INCHES LONG. THAT'S 100,000 FEET OF SPAGHETTI PER DAY, OR 1710 MILES PER SUMMER.

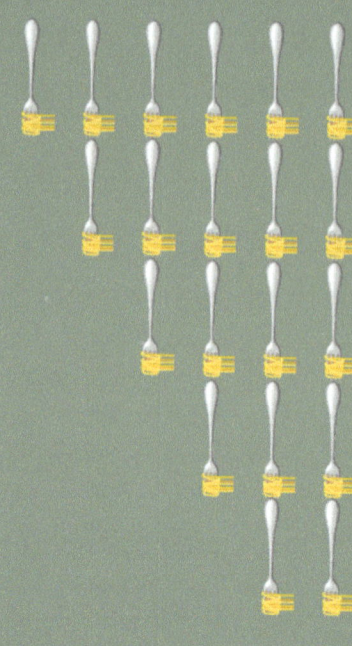
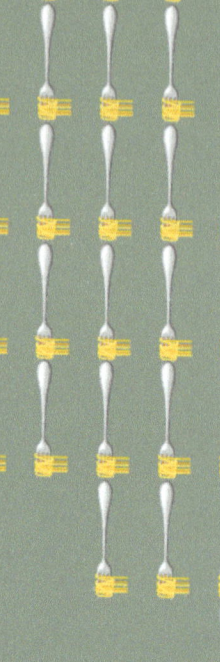
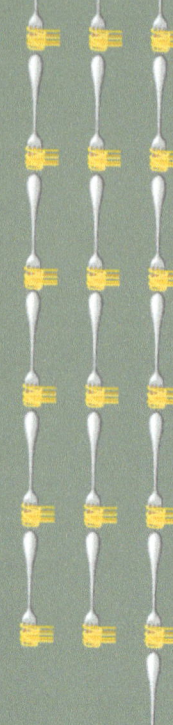
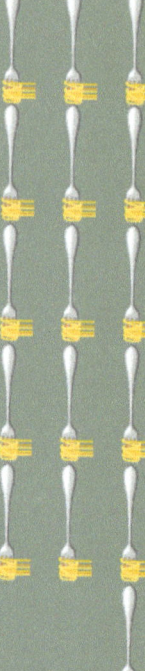
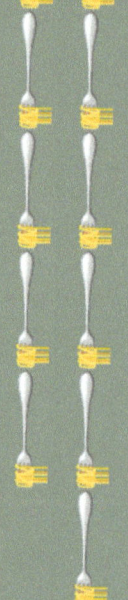
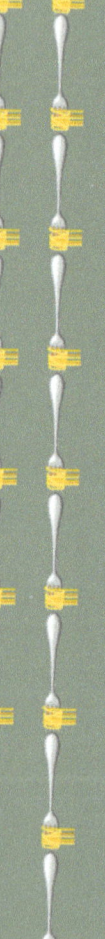

CHELAN TO MANSON: 8 MILES

CHELAN TO WENATCHEE: 39 MILES

CHELAN TO GRAND COULEE DAM: 66 MILES

CHELAN TO SPOKANE: 152 MILES

CHELAN TO SEATTLE: 179 MILES

CHELAN TO VANCOUVER BC: 267 MILES

CHELAN TO PORTLAND: 333 MILES

CHELAN TO BOISE: 438 MILES

CHELAN TO YELLOWSTONE NATIONAL PARK: 627 MILES

CHELAN TO REDWOOD NATIONAL PARK: 650 MILES

CHELAN TO SALT LAKE CITY: 774 MILES

CHELAN TO SAN FRANCISCO: 847 MILES

CHELAN TO LAS VEGAS: 1058 MILES

CHELAN TO DENVER: 1242 MILES

CHELAN TO SAN DIEGO: 1294 MILES

CHELAN TO KANSAS CITY: 1709 MILES

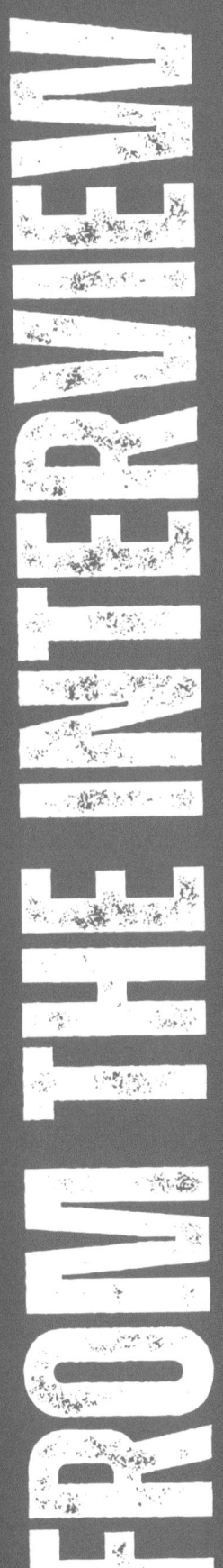

FROM THE INTERVIEW

Lago Pasta

It used to be a karate studio. In the back parking lot, you can actually still see the studio logo on the concrete.

Honestly, this is literally Teague's house. He owns the building and lives upstairs. We joke that when someone sits down and eats here, they're literally sitting down at Teague's table and having dinner in his house.

see page 198 for full interview

Local Myth

PIZZA

Chocolate Torte

INGREDIENTS

- 21 Ounces Dark Chocolate
- 3 ½ Sticks Butter
- 4 Large Eggs
- 2/3 Cup Sugar

DIRECTIONS

Break chocolate into pieces and melt in saucepan with butter gently over low heat. Set aside to cool.

Put eggs & sugar in large bowl and beat with electric mixer until mixture reaches three-times its original volume.

Add 1/4 of melted chocolate into the bowl. Use plastic spatula to mix gently until incorporated. Add remaining chocolate and repeat.

Line a 10-inch cake pan with removable bottom with parchment and butter. Then pour batter into pan. Cook for 8 minutes at 325 degrees. Do not cook for longer.

Remove from the oven and let cool in the pan. Refrigerate for 4 hours or overnight.

Serve with ice cream.

Local Myth Pizza

Lemon Bars

INGREDIENTS

CRUST
- 1/2 Pound Unsalted Butter (Room Temp)
- 1/2 Cup Granulated Sugar
- 2 Cups Flour
- 1/8 Teaspoon Salt

LEMON TOPPING
- 6 Eggs (Room Temp)
- 2 Cups Sugar
- 2 Tablespoons Grated Lemon Zest
- 1 Cup Lemon Juice
- 1 Cup Flour

DIRECTIONS

Recipe makes 2 batches

To make the crust, beat butter and sugar until smooth. Add flour and salt until just thoroughly mixed. Chill in refrigerator. Remove from fridge and divide in half. Roll each half out so that each fits onto 6 1/2 by 8 1/2 inch pan.

Bake crusts at 350 degrees for 15 to 20 minutes.

For topping, whisk all ingredients together and pour over crusts. When both crusts are covered, return them to the oven and continue baking for 10 to 25 minutes until the bars set.

SERVINGS	TIME	DELICIOUSNESS
12	45 mins	10

FROM THE INTERVIEW

january 2024

Caden

If you think about a pizza, it's like building a house. The foundation is the dough and the sauce and the cheese. Then you're putting toppings on. If you can make the best cheese pizza in the world, you're going to have a great pizza, right? Because you've got that foundation.

Bob

This dough here, we age it for 24 hours. What we make today doesn't get used until tomorrow. That aging is called fermentation. It's fermenting and it gets a little more sour as you go. That brings flavor into the dough. The flavor is all about the ingredients and the fermentation: honey, olive oil, flour, sugar, salt, water, yeast.

see page 204 for full interview

Lone Pine

FRUIT STAND

Cherry Almond Pie

GRANDMA JEAN'S CRUST

- 5 Cups All Purpose Flour
- 2 Tablespoons Sugar
- 2 Cups Butter Flavored Crisco
- 1 Stick Salted Butter
- 1 Egg
- 1 Tablespoon Apple Cider Vinegar
- Ice Cold Water

Mix together flour and sugar in a large bowl. Then add the Crisco and salted butter and cut with a pastry cutter until mixed.

Separately, mix together the egg and apple cider vinegar in a measuring cup. Fill with ice cold water until you have one full cup of egg/vinegar/water mixture.

Combine all ingredients. Mix gently into a ball. When you are ready to make your pie, roll the pie crust out and place into a 9-inch deep pie dish. Butter or grease dish beforehand.

If you want to save your pie crust dough for later, it can be frozen until you're ready to make your pie.

Lone Pine Fruit Stand

The Filling

INGREDIENTS

FILLING:

- 5 to 6 Cups Sour Pie Cherries (Sweetened) Fresh or Frozen
- 3 Tablespoons Flour
- 4 Teaspoons Cornstarch
- 4 Teaspoons Tapioca
- 1 Teaspoon Almond Extract
- 1 Teaspoon Lemon Juice

TOPPING:

- 1 Stick Butter (Softened)
- 1 Cup Sugar
- 1 Cup Flour
- 1/2 Cup Toasted Almond Slices

DIRECTIONS

For the filling, mix together all the ingredients in a large bowl. At this point, the desire to sit on the couch and eat this mixture by the spoonful will be overwhelming, but you'll need to control yourself if you want to end up with a finished pie.

Spoon filling into your pie crust (see Grandma Jean's Pie Crust on the previous page).

Next, mix together topping ingredients. Sprinkle topping over the top of the pie filling. Cover the entire top all the way to the edges.

Preheat oven to 400 degrees.

Pop the pie into the oven and bake for 1 hour or until the top is golden brown.

SERVINGS	TIME	DELICIOUSNESS
6	60	10
	mins	

or 1 Roots Middle Schooler

FROM THE INTERVIEW

Lone Pine

This building was originally an apple packing shed. They packed apples here from about 1900 to the 1930s or 1940s. There's still writing on the walls from where they were counting apples as they packed, counting boxes.

Then it changed into picking cabins. They actually put up dividers here and turned it into five cabins. You can see the painted ceiling. Each cabin would have had a living area, bathroom, kitchen, bedroom, all in one square. Very tiny. It stayed that way until 1998. That's when it became a fruit stand.

see page 210 for full interview

Orchard

CAFE

Orchard Cafe

Thai Chicken Noodle Soup

INGREDIENTS

- 1 Tablespoon Vegetable Oil
- 1 Onion (Thinly Sliced)
- 2 Cloves Garlic (Minced)
- 2 Tablespoons Yellow Curry Paste
- 6 Cups Chicken Broth
- 1 15-Ounce Can Coconut Milk
- 1 Tablespoon Fish Sauce
- 2 Red Bell Peppers
- 4 Ounces Thin Rice Noodles
- 2 Skinless Boneless Chicken Breasts (Thinly Sliced Crosswise)
- 1 Tablespoon Fresh Lime Juice
- 1 Cup Roughly Chopped Cilantro
- Salt & Pepper

DIRECTIONS

Heat oil in a large pot. Saute garlic and onion until soft.

Add chicken and cook until lightly browned. Add bell peppers, curry paste and chicken broth. Simmer for 6 to 7 minutes.

Add coconut milk and fish sauce. Bring to low simmer and add noodles (break noodles into pieces first). Cook until noodles are soft.

Add lime juice and garnish with cilantro. Adjust seasoning as desired.

SERVINGS	TIME	DELICIOUSNESS
10	45 mins	10

Molasses Cookies

ORCHARD CAFE

INGREDIENTS

- 1 1/4 Cup Soft Butter
- 2 Cups White Sugar
- 2 Eggs
- 1/2 Cup Molasses
- 4 Cups Flour
- 1/2 Teaspoon Salt
- 4 Teaspoons Baking Soda
- 2 Teaspoons Cinnamon
- 1 Teaspoon Ground Ginger
- 1/2 Teaspoon Ground Clove

DIRECTIONS

Preheat oven to 325 degrees.

Combine butter, 1 cup sugar and the molasses in mixer until creamy. Add egg and mix for 30 seconds. Add remaining dry ingredients and mix for 1 minute.

Chill dough in refrigerator for 45 minutes. Scoop dough into 2-ounce balls and roll in the remaining sugar.

Press balls down onto a parchment-lined sheet pan and bake for 10 to 12 minutes.

Cookie should be soft in the middle and slightly crunchy on the outer edge.

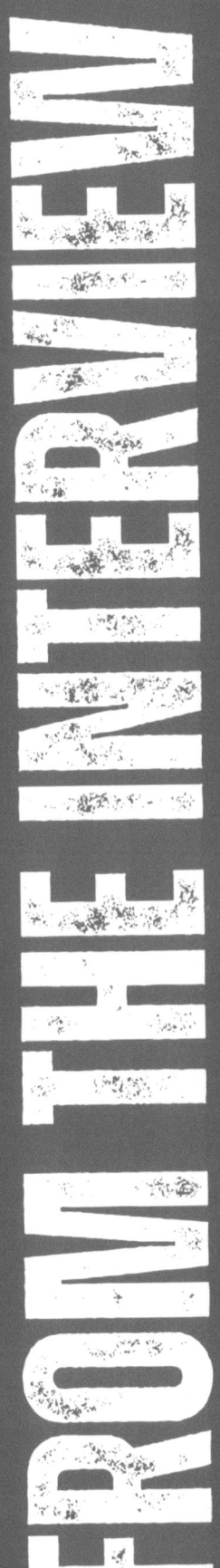

FROM THE INTERVIEW

Orchard Cafe

I love cooking for the patients. When a patient isn't feeling well, I like making them something that's healthy and will make them happy. I like to think I've helped them improve on their condition just a bit. Being at a hospital can be stressful, so it's nice for there to be a space where people can eat really quality food. Hospital food doesn't have the best reputation. It's nice that people can come in and know they're getting a great meal.

see page 221 for full interview

Siren

SONG

Siren Song

Cheesy Cauliflower Dip

INGREDIENTS

- 1 Cup Pancetta or Bacon (Diced)
- 1 Head Cauliflower
- 1 Fresh Fennel Bulb (Thinly Sliced, Base & Stalks Removed)
- 2 Cloves Garlic (Chopped)
- 1/2 Cup Chèvre
- 1/2 Cup Gorgonzola
- 1 Cup Grated Parmigiano-Reggiano
- 1/2 Cup Sour Cream
- 3 Tablespoons Fresh Parsley (Chopped)
- Salt & Pepper
- 3 Tablespoons Breadcrumbs or Panko

DIRECTIONS

Combine cheese & sour cream in large mixing bowl (reserve 3 tablespoons Parmigiano-Reggiano). Set aside.

Slice fennel, chop parsley, & set aside. Break cauliflower florets apart. Chop stem into similarly-sized pieces.

Bring salted water to boil. Add cauliflower. Boil until fork tender (10 to 15 minutes). Drain water and set cauliflower aside.

In large skillet, cook pancetta until lightly browned & crispy. Remove from pan and let drain on paper towel.

Add cauliflower and fennel to the hot pan & drippings. Cook on medium heat until lightly browned. Add garlic. Cook for 2 to 3 minutes.

Combine all ingredients in large bowel, including drippings. Mix gently. Season with salt & pepper.

Transfer mixture to baking dish. Top with breadcrumbs and remaining cheese. Bake at 400 degrees for 15 to 20 minutes.

Serve with crackers or bread.

SERVINGS	TIME	DELICIOUSNESS
4	65 mins	10

Siren Song

Cherry Cordials

INGREDIENTS

- 25 - 30 Pitted Bing Cherries (or 1 Jar of Bada Bing Cherries)
- 12 Ounces Dark Chocolate (70% Cacao)
- Parchment Paper

Recipe requires Fondant (found on next page)

DIRECTIONS

Cherries should be pitted. If using jarred, drain from liquid. Place cherries on baking sheet covered with parchment. Stems should remain. Cherries should not touch each other. Freeze for one to 24 hours.

Apply fondant to cherries (see next page).

Melt chocolate in double boiler. Set up clean sheet pan with fresh parchment. Remove cherries with fondant from the freezer. Hold cherries by stem and dip into chocolate until chocolate covers cherry to the stem. Place on parchment.

Refrigerate dipped cherries until chocolate is firm (about one hour). Cherries taste best when allowed to rest in refrigerator for 24 hours.

Siren Song

Fondant

INGREDIENTS

- 1/4 Cup Butter
- 1/4 Cup Sweetened Condensed Milk
- 3 Cups Confectioner's Sugar
- 4 Teaspoons Vanilla
- Pinch of Salt

DIRECTIONS

Fondant is for use in Siren Song Cherry Cordials

In food processor, combine all ingredients until mixture is completely combined and texture is smooth and tacky to the touch.

If mixture is sticky, add more sugar.

To apply fondant to frozen cherries, remove cherries from the freezer. Work quickly so cherries do not defrost.

Take tablespoon size amount of fondant and roll it between your palms. Make a ball. Flatten ball between your palms and set a cherry stem-up in the middle.

Quickly wrap the disk of fondant up the cherry toward the stem. Fondant should completely cover the cherry but not the stem.

Repeat until all cherries are covered. Return to sheet pan and return the covered cherries to the freezer for one to 24 hours.

SERVINGS	TIME	DELICIOUSNESS
40	10 mins	10

FROM THE INTERVIEW

Siren Song:

We love France and Europe, and we wanted to re-create an experience that reminded us of Bistro life, which is very typical in Europe, where you hang out, have a glass of wine and some food relax and watch the world go by.

The name Siren Song comes from Greek mythology. A Siren Song is an irresistible attraction, it inspires one to think about what they are meant to be or do.

see page 226 for full interview

Vin Du Lac
WINERY

Vin Du Lac Winery

Salmon Ratatouille

INGREDIENTS

- 2 Cups Diced Eggplant
- 2 Cups Diced Zucchini
- 2 Cups Diced Yellow Squash
- 2 Cups Diced Tomatoes
- 1 Cup Diced Onion
- 1 Tablespoon Garlic
- 1.5 Ounces Fresh Basil
- 4 Ounces Fresh Salmon Per Person
- Salt & Pepper to Taste
- 1/3 Cup Olive Oil

DIRECTIONS

In a large skillet over medium-high heat, add olive oil and saute onions, garlic & eggplant until onions are translucent.

Add squash and saute. Season with salt & pepper. Add tomatoes and basil. Lower heat and simmer until tomatoes begin to lose their liquid.

Season salmon with salt & pepper and brush with olive oil. Salmon can be sauteed or grilled to an internal temperature of 145.

To serve, plate ratatouille and place salmon on top of vegetables. Can be served with pasta, rice or on its own.

SERVINGS	TIME	DELICIOUSNESS
4	45 mins	10

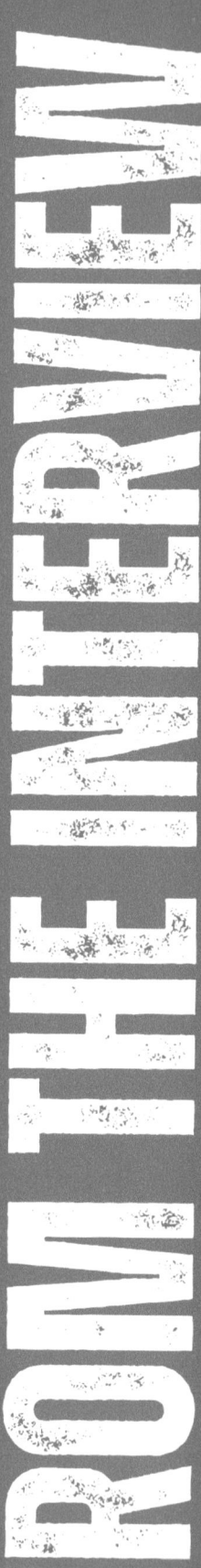

FROM THE INTERVIEW

Vin Du Lac:

I think of our food as fresh Northwest cuisine with French influences. What I mean by that is that we always have fresh produce that we grow here. Any seafood we do we bring in fresh. We focus on foods that are native to the Northwest, salmon and halibut and things that are harvested here.

We also try to use locally raised beef and as much of the local produce as we can. The French influence comes from certain types of dishes and preparations. Our recipes are generally traditional to French classic cooking.

see page 230 for full interview

The Vogue
COFFEE BAR

The Vogue holds a special place in our hearts, as they have hosted our class every Wednesday this year. Every week my 12 middle school students pack into line to order coffee, smoothies, cookies, pastries and sometimes just plain old water. Most customers aren't used to seeing so many middle schoolers together in a coffee shop, and many are rightly surprised to see us outside of school when we ought to be in class studying. But time and again I have had community members pull me aside and make two comments:

1. You come down here for school? It sure wasn't like that when I was a kid!
2. Boy these kids really have excellent manners. Whatever you're doing, keep it up!

A huge thank you to Zack and Mary for allowing us to utilize their business this year as a second classroom and for only putting two shots of coffee in a drink even when one of the kids asks for six.

The Vogue

Lake Chelan Sunrise

INGREDIENTS

- 1/3 Cup Frozen Pineapple
- 1/2 Cup Frozen Mango
- 1/3 Cup Frozen Peaches
- 1/2 Frozen Banana
- Water

DIRECTIONS

Put all ingredients in a blender. Add half a cup of water. Blend on high. Continue adding water until you reach your own desired smoothness.

Best enjoyed just before dawn sitting on the sandy beaches of Lake Chelan while watching the sun come over the eastern mountains.

SERVINGS	TIME	DELICIOUSNESS
I	5 mins	IO

The Vogue

Tropikale Smoothie

INGREDIENTS

- 1/2 Cup Frozen Mango
- 1/2 Cup Frozen Pineapple
- 1 Heaping Teaspoon Ginger Puree
- Greens (Spinach & Kale)
- Water

DIRECTIONS

We prep our smoothies in a 16 oz cold cup so they're ready to go. For the Tropikale, we add the fruit and ginger, then pack the rest of the cup with greens.

Put all ingredients into a blender. Add half cup water. Blend on high. Continue adding water until you reach desired consistency.

SERVINGS	TIME	DELICIOUSNESS
I	5 mins	IO

FULLY CAFFEINATED

In the summer months, The Vogue orders up to 120 pounds of coffee every week from Blue Star Coffee Roasters in Twisp, Washington. Here's how all that coffee breaks down.

480 LBS
of Coffee Beans
Per Month

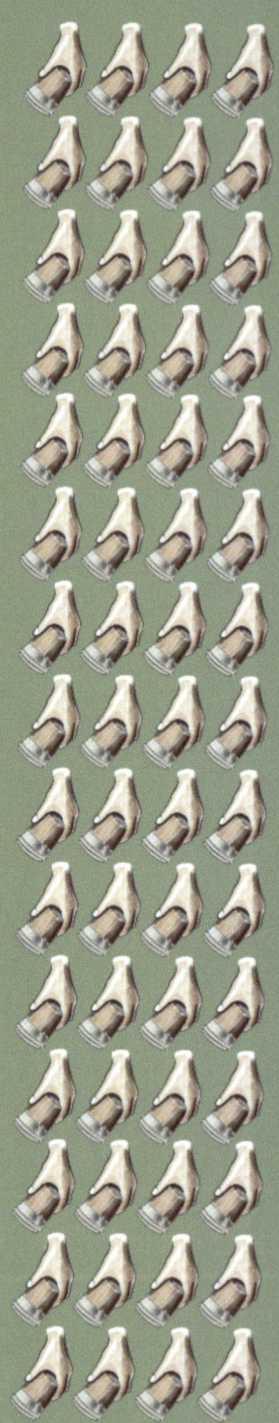

217,440 Grams
of Coffee Per
Month

13,600
Drinks Per
Month

1,698,750 Mg
of Caffeine
Per Month

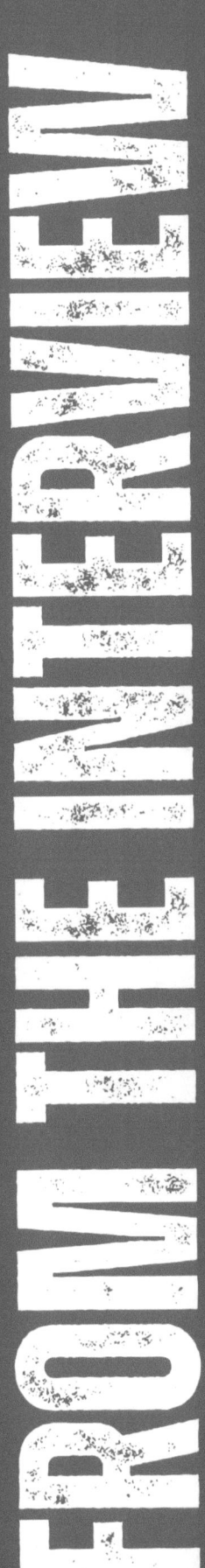

FROM THE INTERVIEW

Vogue:

Yeah, like we bought a La Marzocco espresso machine. It was the first one of that model in North America to be installed. The owner of Blue Star Coffee encouraged us to get that, and it makes a big difference in the quality of the espresso. Total game changer.

The Vogue always made good coffee, but we've really tried to up the game. We're always trying to improve, you know?

see page 236 for full interview

COMMUNITY RECIPES

Ronald Earvin

Apple Crisp

INGREDIENTS

- 1 Box Refrigerated Pie Crusts (Softened)
- 1 Cup Sugar
- 3 Tablespoons Flour
- 2 Tablespoons Cinnamon
- 1/4 Teaspoon Nutmeg
- 1/4 Teaspoon Salt
- 1 1/2 Tablespoon Lemon Juice
- 12 Cups Thinly Sliced Apples (Peeled)
- 1 Cup Powdered Sugar
- 2 Tablespoons Milk

DIRECTIONS

Heat oven to 450 degrees. Remove pie crusts from pouches. Unroll and stack crusts one on top of the other on lightly floured surface. Roll to 17 x 12 inch pan, pressing into corners. Fold extra pastry crust until even with edges of the pan and crimp edges.

Mix sugar, flour, cinnamon, nutmeg, salt & lemon juice. Stir in apples to coat. Spoon apple mixture into crust-lined pan.

Bake 33 to 38 minutes or until crust is golden brown and filling is bubbling.

Cool on rack for 45 minutes.

Mix powdered sugar and milk until well blended. Drizzle over apples. Allow glaze to set before serving, about 30 minutes.

Cuts best with a pizza wheel.

SERVINGS	TIME	DELICIOUSNESS
12	180 mins	10

INGREDIENTS

FOR THE MEATLOAF:

- 1 Pound Ground Beef
- 1/2 Pound Regular Sausage
- 1 Egg
- 1 Cup Breadcrumbs
- 1/2 Cup Applesauce
- 2 Tablespoons Chopped Onions
- 1 Tablespoon Dijon Mustard
- 2 Tablespoons Worcestershire
- 1 Teaspoon Garlic Powder
- Salt & Pepper

FOR THE SAUCE:

- 1/2 Cup Applesauce
- 1 Teaspoon Dijon Mustard
- 1 Tablespoon Brown Sugar
- 1 Tablespoon Apple Cider Vinegar
- 1 Teaspoon Allspice
- 1 Teaspoon Cinnamon

Inspired by Nancy Williams

Applesauce Meatloaf

DIRECTIONS

Preheat oven to 350 degrees.

Mix together ingredients for meatloaf. If consistency of meat seems too wet, add more breadcrumbs. Then shape meat in a loaf pan.

Place pan into the oven. Bake for 20 minutes. While baking, combine ingredients for sauce. Remove meatloaf and smother in sauce.

Return to oven for 20 to 30 minutes.

SERVINGS	TIME	DELICIOUSNESS	
2	70 mins	10	84

Inspired by Jeanette Grant

Apple Zucchini Bread

INGREDIENTS

- 1 3/4 Cups Flour
- 2 Teaspoons Cinnamon
- 1 Teaspoon Baking Soda
- 1/2 Teaspoon Salt
- 2 Teaspoons Allspice
- 2 Teaspoons Nutmeg
- 1 Teaspoon Ground Ginger
- 1 Cup Applesauce
- 1/3 Cup Coconut Oil
- 3/4 Cup Light Brown Sugar
- 1/4 Cup White Sugar
- 2 Eggs
- 2 Teaspoons Vanilla
- 1 1/2 Cups Shredded Zucchini
- 1 Cup Apples (Peeled & Chopped)
- 1/2 Cup Walnuts (Chopped)

DIRECTIONS

Preheat oven to 350 degrees.

In a medium bowl, combine flour, one teaspoon cinnamon, baking soda, salt, allspice, nutmeg, and ginger. Set aside.

In a separate bowl, combine applesauce, coconut oil, brown sugar, white sugar, eggs, and vanilla. Mix together and then stir in the zucchini.

Combine dry ingredients with the wet ingredients and stir.

In a separate bowl, combine apples with remaining cinnamon.

Mix apples and walnuts gently into the batter.

Pour batter into a loaf pan. Cook in oven for 50 to 60 minutes.

SERVINGS	TIME	DELICIOUSNESS
6	80 mins	10

Morgan Fraser

Audrey's Apple Pie

INGREDIENTS

- 2 Single Uncooked Pie Crusts
  (see Audrey's Pie Crust)
- 5 Large Golden Delicious Apples
  (Cored, Peeled & Sliced)
- 1 Cup Sugar
- 1 Teaspoon Cinnamon
- 3 Tablespoons Butter

DIRECTIONS

Preheat oven to 425 degrees.

Carefully place uncooked pie crust in 9-inch pie pan. Fill with sliced apples.

Sprinkle cinnamon and sugar over the apples. Divide butter into 10 small pieces and place on top of apple mixture.

Roll out the second pie crust. Place it over the apples and cut off all but about a 3/4 inch of dough around the edges. Seal with fingers or fork.

Cut diagonal slits in the top of the crust for venting. Brush top with milk and sprinkle with a little sugar.

Bake for 15 minutes at 425 degrees. Then lower temperature to 350 degrees and bake for 1 hour or until golden brown.

Serve with vanilla ice cream or fresh whipped cream.

SERVINGS	TIME	DELICIOUSNESS
6	95 mins	10

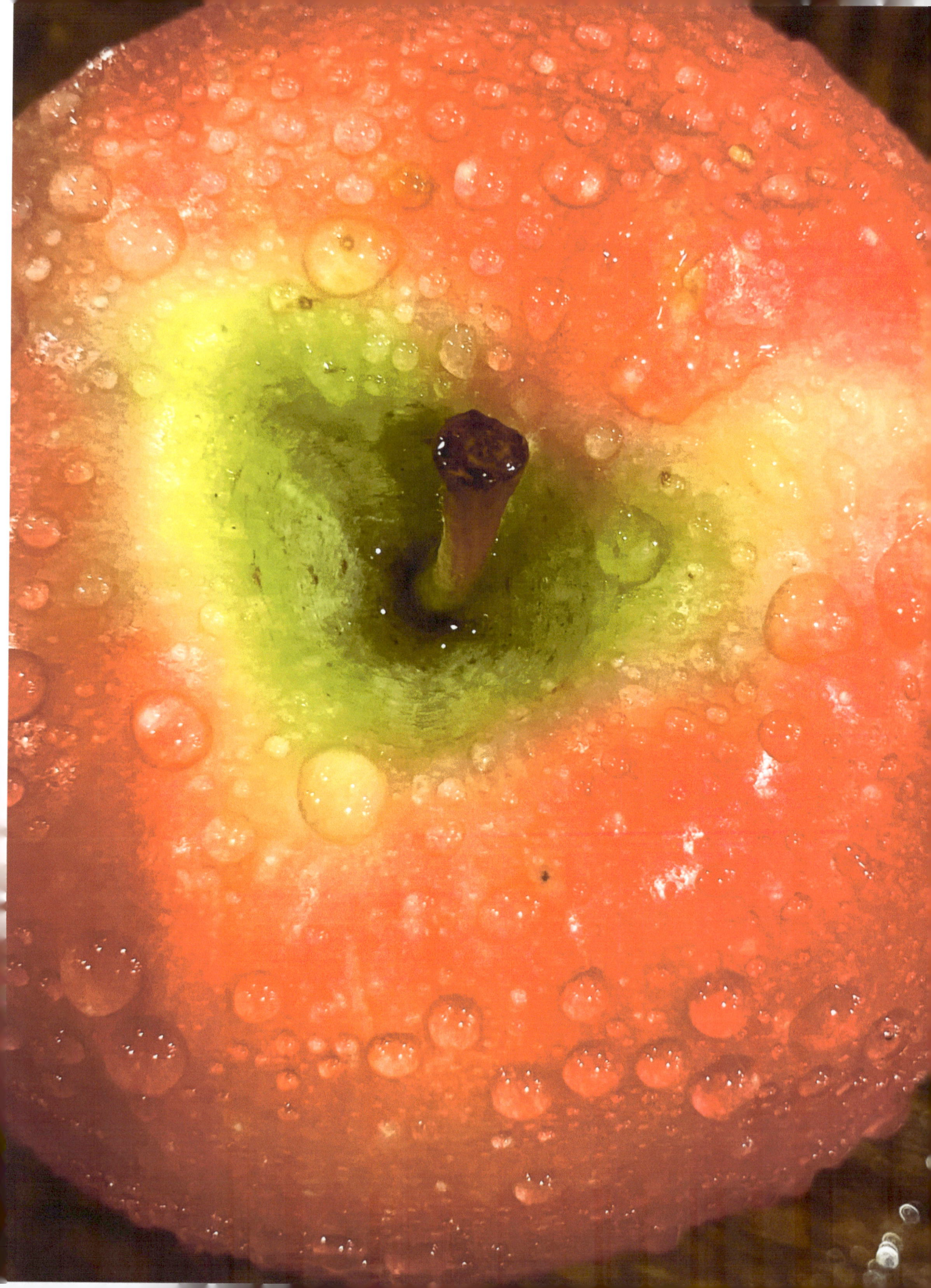

Morgan Fraser

Audrey's Pie Crust

INGREDIENTS

- 2 & 1/3 Cups All Purpose Flour
- 1 Teaspoon Salt
- 1 Cup Crisco
- 1 Egg
- 1 & 1/2 Teaspoons Cider Vinegar
- 1/4 Cup Cold Water

DIRECTIONS

Combine flour, salt and Crisco in large bowl. Blend with a pastry blender, pastry cutter or knives until crumbly.

In a small bowl, whisk together egg, cider vinegar and water. Drizzle over the flour mixture and mix thoroughly. Dough will be soft and a little sticky. If it's too sticky, add more flour.

Shape dough into two patties. Wrap in plastic wrap and place in freezer for 45 minutes.

When ready to make your pie, take one patty out of the fridge and roll it out on a floured surface. Crust should be slightly larger than the pie pan. When you're finished with one crust, repeat the process with the second crust.

SERVINGS	TIME	DELICIOUSNESS
2	65 mins	10

Heidi Ildhuso

Brussel Sprout Salad

INGREDIENTS

FOR THE SALAD:
- 1 1/2 Pounds Brussel Sprouts
- 1 Cup Diced Apple
- 1/2 Cup Crumbled Feta or Blue Cheese
- 1/2 Cup Pomegranate Arils
- 1/2 Cup Bacon (Cooked & Crumbled)
- 1 Cup Walnuts Roughly Chopped

FOR THE SALAD
- 1 Tablespoon Minced Shallot
- 1/3 Cup Olive Oil
- 2 Tablespoons Red Wine Vinegar
- 2 Teaspoons Dijon
- 2 Teaspoons Honey
- Salt & Pepper to Taste

DIRECTIONS

Cut off the ends of the Brussel sprouts, and then cut in half lengthwise. Thinly slice sprouts crosswise to cut into shreds.

Place the shredded Brussel sprouts in a bowl. Add apple, cheese, walnuts, pomegranate, and bacon. Mix together.

For the dressing, combine shallot, olive oil, red wine vinegar, salt and pepper in mason jar. Shake well.

Pour dressing over the salad. Toss to combine.

SERVINGS	TIME	DELICIOUSNESS
6	20 mins	10

Doug & Sue Perry

Buttermilk Biscuits

INGREDIENTS

- 4 Cups All Purpose Flour
- 1 Teaspoon Baking Soda
- 2 Tablespoons Baking Powder
- 2 Tablespoons Granulated Sugar
- 1 Teaspoon Salt
- 1 1/2 Sticks Unsalted Butter (Cold)
- 1 1/2 Cups Buttermilk

DIRECTIONS

Preheat oven to 425 degrees.

Place butter in freezer for 15 to 20 minutes before adding to mixture. Line baking pans with parchment paper. Sprinkle prep surface with extra flour.

Mix dry ingredients in a large bowl and set aside. Grate the very cold butter into dry mixture. Combine butter into flour mix with pastry cutter where butter has a coarse almost crumb-like texture. Butter should be pea-sized. Do not over-mix.

Add buttermilk, incorporating with wooden spoon. Mix just to moisten dry ingredients. Do not over-mix.

Turn dough onto prep surface. using hands, flatten dough to 1-inch thickness (no rolling pins). Fold mixture over itself and flatten again with hands. Turn dough one quarter turn and repeat. Do this four times & flatten to 1-inch thickness.

Cut dough into biscuits with biscuit cutter. Place on baking pan 1/4 to 1/2 inch apart.

Bake at 425 for 5 minutes. Then brush tops with butter & return to oven for 5 minutes or until golden brown.

SERVINGS	TIME	DELICIOUSNESS
16	60 mins	10

Tyler Miller

Carrot Top Pesto Pasta

INGREDIENTS

- 1/2 Cup Pine Nuts
- 5 Garlic Cloves
- Juice From Half a Lemon
- 2 to 3 Cups of Carrot Top Greens
- 1/2 Cup Olive Oil
- 1/2 Cup Grated Parmesan Cheese
- Salt & Pepper
- 1 Bag Radiatori Pasta from Lago Pasta

DIRECTIONS

To make the pesto, combine pine nuts, garlic, lemon juice, carrot top greens (stems can be included), olive oil, parmesan, salt and pepper (to taste) in a food processor.

Blend well.

Everyone likes their pesto sauce a little different. Feel free to add more or less of any ingredient until the taste and consistency is to your liking. If the sauce is too chunky, add more olive oil. If it tastes too sour, add more cheese and pine nuts.

For the pasta, bring a large pot of heavily salted water to boil. Add radiatori. If using fresh radiatori from Pasta Lago, cook time should be between 2 and 5 minutes depending upon how well done you like your pasta.

Drain water from pasta. Add pesto sauce directly to pot and stir.

Serve with additional parmesan sprinkled over the top.

SERVINGS	TIME	DELICIOUSNESS
4	20 mins	10

Melody Murray

Chelan Sun Tea

INGREDIENTS

- 1 Large Glass Tea Jar Filled With Fresh Lake Chelan Water
- 8 Packets Lipton Black Tea
- 3/4 Cup White Sugar
- Sliced Lemons (If Desired)

DIRECTIONS

Early in the morning, fill glass tea jar with cold water. Add packets of Lipton tea. Tighten lid on jar.

Find a place in your yard that receives sunlight throughout the day. You may need to move your jar to keep it in the sunlight. Leave jar in the sunshine until late in the afternoon (4:00 or later).

Remove jar from sun. While still warm, add sugar and stir to incorporate.

Cool tea in fridge or pour over ice and serve. Add wedges of lemon if desired.

I do not recommend leaving the tea in the sealed jar. It will begin to take on a funky taste. Flavor remains best when tea is transferred to an open pitcher and placed in fridge.

SERVINGS	TIME	DELICIOUSNESS
8	8 *hours*	10

Inspired by Jan M.

Chili-Roast Chicken

INGREDIENTS

- 1/2 Cup Plain Chobani Greek Yogurt
- 1 Teaspoon Cinnamon
- 1 Teaspoon Chili Powder
- 2 Teaspoons Paprika
- 1 Teaspoon Sriracha
- 4 Cloves Garlic (Minced)
- Juice of 1/2 Small Lemon
- 1 Tablespoon Salt
- 2 Teaspoons Black Pepper
- 1 Roasting Chicken (3 lbs) Quartered

DIRECTIONS

In large baking dish, mix all ingredients except the chicken.

Add chicken and coat with marinade mixture. Cover tightly and marinate in refrigerator overnight.

When ready to cook, preheat oven to 500 degrees.

Place chicken on raised broiler rack and place it in the oven. Immediately reduce heat to 350 degrees and roast for roughly 1 and 1/4 hours.

When done, remove skin from chicken if preferred.

Serve hot or cold.

SERVINGS	TIME	DELICIOUSNESS
4	90 mins	10

INGREDIENTS

- 1 Cup Milk
- 1 Cup Boiling Water
- 3/4 Cup Sugar
- 1/2 Teaspoon Salt
- 1 Teaspoon Vanilla
- 1/2 Cup Cocoa Powder
- 2 Tablespoons Flour
- 1/4 Cup Butter
- Chili Powder to Taste

Inspired by Patty Etzkorn

Chocolate Gravy

DIRECTIONS

Melt butter in a saucepan and add flour. Whisk and continue whisking until mixture browns slightly.

Add sugar and salt. Keep whisking so mixture doesn't burn. Add cocoa powder and chili powder and stir. Add boiling water and stir until smooth. Add milk and stir.

Let mixture get hot <u>but not boil</u>. Stir until it thickens. If bubbles start to appear, remove from heat. Add vanilla and stir to incorporate.

Serve over buttermilk biscuits or pancakes.

SERVINGS	TIME	DELICIOUSNESS
6	20 mins	10

Inspired by Tom Tedor

Cinema Blend Popcorn

INGREDIENTS

- 10 Cups Popped Popcorn
- 1 Cup Roasted Peanuts
- 8 Cups Plain Chex Cereal
- 5 Cups Mini Pretzels
- 3 Cups M&Ms
- 1`/2 Teaspoon Vanilla
- 1/2 Cup Butter
- 1 Cup Dark Brown Sugar
- 1/2 Cup Light Corn Syrup
- 1/4 Teaspoon Baking Soda

DIRECTIONS

Toss together popcorn, peanuts, Chex, and pretzels in a large roasting pan.

In a saucepan, melt butter in saucepan. Add brown sugar and corn syrup. Bring to boil and stir constantly so mixture doesn't burn.

After five minutes, remove from heat. Add baking soda and vanilla. Stir until smooth.

Pour corn syrup mixture over popcorn in roasting pan. Toss to coat.

Bake at 250 degrees for 1 hour, stirring every 15 minutes.

Remove from heat and cool. Break into small clusters. Add M&Ms right before serving.

SERVINGS	TIME	DELICIOUSNESS
10	75 mins	10

Creamy Tartar Sauce

INSPIRED BY KAY SIKES

INGREDIENTS

- 1 Cup Real Mayo
- 2 Tablespoons Minced Onion
- 2 Tablespoons Sliced Pimento
- 1 Small Dill Pickle (Finely Shredded)
- 2 Tablespoons Chopped Fresh Parsley
- 2 Tablespoons Chopped Fresh Dill
- Juice of 1 Small Lemon
- Salt and Pepper to Taste

INSTRUCTIONS

Mix all ingredients together. Chill.

Serve with fish and chips or chicken strips.

Gordon LaChance

Derby Pie

INGREDIENTS

- 3 Eggs
- 1 1/2 Cups Dark Brown Sugar
- 3/4 Cups Melted Butter
- 3/4 Cups Flour
- 1 Cup Dark Chocolate Chips
- 1/2 Cup Milk Chocolate Chips
- 1 1/2 Cups Walnuts
- 3 Tablespoons Blue Spirits Straight Bourbon Whisky
- 1 Tablespoon Vanilla
- 1 Graham Cracker Crust Pie Shell

DIRECTIONS

Preheat oven to 350 degrees.

Using a mixer, beat eggs. Then gradually add dark sugar, butter, and flour until combined.

Stir in chocolate chips, walnuts, Blue Spirits bourbon whisky, and vanilla.

Pour pie mixture into graham cracker crust and bake for 40 minutes.

SERVINGS	TIME	DELICIOUSNESS
6	60 mins	10

INGREDIENTS

- 1 Pound Ground Beef
- 1/2 Cup Chopped Scallions
- 1 Packet Beef Taco Seasoning
- Salt, Pepper & Garlic Powder
- 4 Ounce Can Chopped Green Chilies
- 2 Cups Milk
- 1 1/3 Cup Bisquick Baking Mix
- 4 Eggs
- 2 Roma Tomatoes (Chopped)
- 1 Head of Lettuce (Shredded)
- 2 Cups Mexican Cheese
- Sour Cream
- 1 Can El Pato Tomato Sauce (Optional)
- 1 Lime

Inspired by Pat Oestreich

Easy Taco Pie

DIRECTIONS

Heat oven to 400 degrees. Grease 10 x 11 inch pie pan.

Cook ground beef on stove. Add taco seasoning, salt, pepper, and garlic powder to taste. Add scallions and green chilies (drain first). Spread mixture on bottom of the pie pan.

Beat milk, eggs, and Bisquick together until smooth. Pour over meat mixture. Bake for 35 minutes.

Remove pie pan from oven. Top with chopped tomatoes and cheese. Return to oven until cheese is melted. Remove from oven again and top with shredded lettuce.

For heat, drizzle with El Pato tomato sauce. Serve with sour cream and wedge of lime.

SERVINGS
6

TIME
60
mins

DELICIOUSNESS
10

101

Fried Apples

DON ALLEN

INGREDIENTS

- 6 Tart Granny Smith Apples
- 1/2 Stick Butter
- 2 to 4 Tablespoons Brown Sugar

INSTRUCTIONS

Peel, core and slice apples.

In a cast iron skillet, melt two tablespoons of butter in order to coat the pan.

Saute the sliced apples on low/medium heat until tender. This may take up to 15 to 20 minutes. Stir apples to prevent burning. Continue adding butter as the apples cook.

When apples are soft enough to poke a fork through them easily, add the brown sugar. Cook until brown sugar is melted and syrupy.

Enjoy!

Goochi's Black Bean Chili

 6 servings   Overnight

INGREDIENTS

- 1 Cup Dried Black Beans (Soaked Overnight)
- 1-1/2 Cups Diced Onion
- 1-1/2 Cups Diced Green Pepper
- 3/4 Cup Diced Celery
- 1-1/4 lb. Cubed Sirloin
- 3/4 Cup Olive Oil
- 1/4 Cup Flour
- 1-1/2 Teaspoon Thyme
- 1-1/2 Teaspoon Cumin
- 1/4 Teaspoon Pepper
- 1/4 Teaspoon Red Chili Flakes
- 1-1/2 Teaspoon Minced Garlic
- 2 Tablespoons Granulated Onion
- 1/4 Teaspoon Cayenne Pepper
- 2 Cups Water
- 2 Tablespoons Beef Base (Or 1 Beef Bouillon Cube)
- 1 Teaspoon Tabasco
- 1 Tablespoon Worcestershire
- 3 Cups Puréed Canned Tomatoes
- 4 oz Diced Green Chilies

DIRECTIONS

Soak the beans overnight.

Dice onions, green pepper and celery. Cut sirloin into small cubes and set aside.

Prepare the roux by whisking in a small saucepan 1/4 cup of olive oil and 1/4 cup flour on medium heat. When browned, stir 1/4 cup diced onions and set aside to cool.

In a large pot on medium heat, add 1/2 cup diced onions and 1/2 cup olive oil. Stir until dark brown but not burned.

Add to the pot: thyme, cumin, pepper, chili flakes, minced garlic, granulated onion, cayenne pepper, 1/2 cup diced onion and 1 cup green pepper.

Then add: water, beef base (or bouillon cube), Tabasco, Worcestershire, canned tomatoes, diced celery, and diced green chilies. Mix well and simmer.

Rinse off and drain beans. Add the roux, 1/4 cup onion, and 1/2 cup green pepper. Stir together and then mix into pot and bring to boil.

Serve hot.

Goochi's

Goochi's Clam Chowder

INGREDIENTS

- 3/4 Pound Bacon (Chopped)
- 5 Red Potatoes (Diced)
- 2 Cups Onions (Diced)
- 1 Teaspoon Thyme
- 1 Teaspoon Basil
- 1 Teaspoon Italian Seasoning
- 2 Bay Leaves
- 1 Tablespoon Granulated Onion
- Dash of Tabasco
- 2 Cans Diced Clams
- 1 Pint Half & Half
- 1/2 Cup Butter
- 1/2 Cup Flour
- Chopped Parsley (Optional)

DIRECTIONS

In a large pot, saute bacon on medium heat until done. Do not drain.

Add potatoes, onions, seasonings, and Tabasco. Cook while stirring for 5 minutes.

Add clams with juice and bring to boil.

Prepare a roux by melting butter in a small saucepan on medium high heat. Add flour gradually and whisk until thickened.

Stir roux and half & half into the large pot with vegetables and clams. Stir well. If necessary to thin, add milk.

Remove bay leaves and serve hot with chopped parsley on top.

SERVINGS	TIME	DELICIOUSNESS
2	30 mins	10

Goochi Mushrooms

GOOCHI'S

INGREDIENTS

- 12 Whole Mushrooms
- 1 Oz Butter
- Steak Seasoning
- 2 Ozs White Wine
- 1 Oz Teriyaki Sauce
- 1 1/2 Teaspoon Garlic Butter

INSTRUCTIONS

In medium saute pan, place mushrooms in butter and toss to coat. Sprinkle with steak seasoning.

Saute on high heat. Keep turning until seasoning begins to burn onto the mushrooms.

Add white wine, then Teriyaki sauce. Finish with garlic butter.

Toss until butter is melted and sauce clings to mushrooms.

Cora Clark

Grandma Cora's Aplets

INGREDIENTS

- 1 1/2 Cups Unsweetened Apple Sauce
- 4 Cups Sugar
- 4 Packages Knox Gelatin
- 1/4 Teaspoon Salt
- 1/2 Cup Water
- 1 Cup Walnuts
- 1 Teaspoon Vanilla
- Confectioners Sugar

DIRECTIONS

Mix apple sauce, sugar, gelatin, salt, and water together in à boil. Then pour into saucepan and bring to a boil. Simmer for 20 minutes.

Add walnuts and vanilla.

Pour into a flat pan and let stand overnight.

In the morning, cut into squares and roll in confectioners sugar.

SERVINGS
50+

TIME
OVERNIGHT

DELICIOUSNESS
10

Grilled Sockeye Salmon

 1 serving   10 minutes

INGREDIENTS

- One Sockeye Salmon (Less Than One Inch Thick)
- Garlic Salt
- 2 Tablespoons Brown Sugar
- 1/4 Cube Butter

You will need a hinged wire fish clamp & aluminum foil.

DIRECTIONS

Preheat grill to 400 degrees. Melt butter in microwave and mix with brown sugar.

Lay aluminum foil on fish clamp lengthwise. Foil needs to be long enough at both ends so you can bring them together and fold over the fish. For now, roll those long ends loosely so that when you close the fish clamp, the fish does not get covered.

Place fish on foil with skin side down. Brush butter/sugar mixture on flesh side and sprinkle with garlic salt. Close clamp and place on open fire so flesh side is on the fire. Leave cooking at 400 degrees for 3 minutes.

Remove from fire. Open clamp. Brush again with butter/sugar mix. Sprinkle with garlic salt. Unroll the extra foil at the ends and place over the fish to make a pouch. Seal edges.

Reduce heat to 350 degrees. Place pouch on grill with flesh side up (top of pouch). Cook 6 minutes or until fish flakes have separated.

Note that fish will continue to cook as long as it is in the pouch.

Heidi's Pea Salad

HEIDI ILDHUSO

INGREDIENTS

- 3 Packages English Peas (Trader Joes)
- 10 Strips Bacon (Cooked & Chopped)
- 1 Cup Shredded Cheddar Jack Cheese
- 1 Can Water Chestnuts (Drained & Cut in Half)
- Fresh Black Pepper
- 1 Cup Mayo
- 1 Cup Sour Cream
- 1/2 Teaspoon Cayenne Pepper
- 1/2 Teaspoon Paprika

INSTRUCTIONS

Combine English peas, chopped bacon, cheese and water chestnuts in a large bowl. Add pepper to taste.

For dressing, combine mayo and sour cream. Mix together. Then add cayenne, paprika, salt and pepper. Whip together until combined.

Add dressing to salad as desired.

Ronald Earvin

Holy Smoke Baked Beans

INGREDIENTS

- 8 Slices Bacon
- 1 Medium White Onion (Chopped)
- 1/2 Green Pepper (Chopped)
- 3 (28-Oz) Cans Pork & Beans
- 1 Cup Barbecue Sauce
- 3/4 Cup Brown Sugar
- 1/2 Cup Apple Cider Vinegar
- 3 Tablespoons Dijon
- 1 Tablespoon Ketchup
- 1 Tablespoon Smoked Paprika
- 4 Garlic Cloves (Minced)
- Salt & Pepper

DIRECTIONS

Preheat oven to 325 degrees.

Cut bacon into fourths. Fry bacon in a pan until about half cooked so that there is a good amount of drippings in the pan. Remove bacon and set aside.

Add onion and green pepper to the pan and saute in the bacon drippings.

Once onions are translucent, add remaining ingredients to the pan and bring to a simmer.

Pour the bean mixture into an oven pan. Smooth out and top with bacon.

Place the pan into the oven and cook for 2 hours.

SERVINGS	TIME	DELICIOUSNESS
12	140 mins	10

Beckitt Eloise

Lake Burger

INGREDIENTS

THE BURGER

- 1 Pound Hamburger (90% Lean)
- 1/2 Pound Plain Sausage
- 1 Egg
- 2 Tablespoons Worcestershire
- 1/4 Cup Heavy Cream
- 1 Tablespoon Garlic Powder
- 1 Tablespoon Italian Seasoning
- 1/2 Cup Breadcrumbs
- Salt & Pepper
- Buns

SMOKEY SAUCE

- 1/2 Cup Mayo
- 1/2 Cup Ketchup
- 1 Tablespoon Worcestershire
- Smoked Paprika
- Salt & Pepper

DIRECTIONS

In large bowl, mix hamburger and sausage together. Add egg, Worcestershire, heavy cream, garlic powder and Italian seasoning. Add salt and pepper to taste. Stir to combine.

Add breadcrumbs to meat mixture. Add additional breadcrumbs if necessary until meat mixture is no longer slick and wet.

Form meat into burger patties of desired size.

Heat grill up to 400 degrees. Cook burger patties to desired doneness.

As burgers cook, make Smokey Sauce by combining all ingredients and whisking together. Adjust paprika, salt and pepper to taste. Sauce should be slightly tangy and smokey.

Burgers can be served on cold buns, or buns can be lathered in butter, seasoned with salt and pepper, and grilled face-down until browned.

Burgers will be juicy. I recommend using thick buns that will absorb the liquid as you eat.

SERVINGS	TIME	DELICIOUSNESS
4 - 6	25 mins	10

INGREDIENTS

- 3 Cups Flour
- 3 Teaspoons Baking Powder
- 1 Teaspoon Salt
- 1/2 Cup Sugar
- 12 Ounces Manson Beach Blonde from Lake Chelan Brewery
- 1/2 Cup Melted Butter

Inspired by Paula & Tom Kunkel

Lakeside Beer Bread

DIRECTIONS

Preheat oven to 375 degrees.

Mix dry ingredients and beer. Be sure to sift flour. If you do not have a sifter, then spoon the flour from the bag into the measuring cup (dipping the cup into the bag and leveling it off compacts the flour).

Pour into greased loaf pan. Pour melted butter over mixture. Bake for one hour.

SERVINGS
6

TIME
75
mins

DELICIOUSNESS
10

113

Inspired by Tara Hensley

Maple Banana Bread

INGREDIENTS

FOR THE BREAD:

- 1 1/2 Cup Sugar
- 2 Cups Flour
- 1 Teaspoon Salt
- 1 Teaspoon Baking Soda
- 1/2 Cup Vegetable Oil
- 2 Mashed Bananas
- 1 Cup Chopped Pecans
- 1 Teaspoon Vinegar
- 3 1/2 Tablespoons Milk
- 2 Eggs

FOR THE MAPLE GLAZE:

- 1/4 Cup Butter
- 1/2 Cup Pure Maple Syrup
- 1/4 Teaspoon Cinnamon
- 1/2 Teaspoon Vanilla
- 1 Cup Powdered Sugar

DIRECTIONS

Preheat oven to 350 degrees.

For the bread, mix all ingredients together in a large bowl. Stir until smooth. Pour into loaf pan and bake for 75 minutes.

Remove from oven and let cool.

While bread is cooling, melt butter on the stove in a saucepan. Add maple syrup, cinnamon, and vanilla. Stir to combine and then remove from heat.

Sift in powdered sugar and whisk to combine. Then let glaze cool for 10 minutes.

Once glaze has thickened, stir it up and drizzle over the top of the banana bread. Allow glaze to harden.

Serve and enjoy.

SERVINGS	TIME	DELICIOUSNESS
6	90 *mins*	10

Inspired by Yesterday's Pizza

Margherita Pizza Sub

INGREDIENTS

FOR THE SAUCE:

- 1 Can San Marzano Crushed Tomatoes
- 4 Cloves Garlic (Minced)
- 1 Tablespoon Olive Oil
- 1 Teaspoon Sugar
- Salt & Pepper

FOR THE PIZZA:

- 1 Loaf French Bread
- 1 Package Fresh Basil
- 1 Package Fresh Mozzarella
- 5 Tablespoons Parmigiano-Reggiano Cheese
- Red Pepper Flakes
- Olive Oil

DIRECTIONS

Preheat oven to 350 degrees.

For the sauce, mix all ingredients and stir. Add salt and pepper to taste. Set aside.

Cut French loaf lengthwise down the middle to separate into two long sections. Brush each section lightly with olive oil. Sprinkle with salt and pepper.

Spread pizza sauce over each half of the loaf. Add whole basil leaves.

Slice mozzarella into tiny cubes and place atop pizza sauce. Then sprinkle parmigiano-reggiano cheese on top. Add red pepper flakes as desired.

Bake in oven until mozzarella cheese is melted. After removing from oven, drizzle lightly with olive oil. Cut into sections and serve.

SERVINGS	TIME	DELICIOUSNESS
4	30 mins	10

Inspired by Greta Griffiths

Marinated Turkey Salad

INGREDIENTS

FOR DRESSING:

- 5 Cloves Garlic (Minced)
- 1/4 Cup Extra Virgin Olive Oil
- 1/4 Cup Red Wine Vinegar
- Juice of 1 Lemon
- 2 Tablespoons Dried Oregano
- 1 Tablespoon Dried Marjoram
- 1 Tablespoon Dijon
- 1 Teaspoon Honey
- Salt and Pepper to Taste

FOR SALAD:

- 6 Cups Diced Cooked Turkey
- 3 Cups Green Grapes (Or Pineapple Bits)
- 2 1/2 Cups Diced Celery
- 1 Can Crispy Chinese Noodles
- 2 Cups Cashew Nuts
- Mayo as Needed
- Lettuce Leaves

DIRECTIONS

For dressing, mix all ingredients together and blend with immersion blender.

When dressing is complete, pour over the turkey. Marinate overnight and drain the next day.

Just before serving, mix all the other ingredients together.

To moisten the salad, add mayo that is slightly diluted with water. Amount of mayo will depend on how moist you want the salad.

To serve, mound onto lettuce leaves. Serve with hot rolls.

SERVINGS	TIME	DELICIOUSNESS
12	20 mins	10

Inspired by Joye Meyer

No Peekie Oven Stew

INGREDIENTS

- 3 Pounds Stew Meat
- 2 Yellow Onions (Sliced)
- 1 Cup Diced Celery
- 5 Russet Potatoes (Chopped)
- 4 Carrots (Chopped)
- 1 Tablespoon Sugar
- 2 Tablespoons Salt
- 1 Tablespoon Pepper
- 7 Cloves Garlic (Smashed)
- 2 Tablespoons Balsamic Vinegar
- 1 1/2 Tablespoons Tomato Paste
- 1/4 Cup Flour
- 2 Cups Dry Red Wine
- 2 Cups Beef Broth
- 2 Cups Water
- 1 Bay Leaf
- 2 Teaspoons Dried Thyme
- 3 Tablespoons Olive Oil
- Chopped Parsley

DIRECTIONS

Preheat oven to 250 degrees. On stovetop, melt some butter in a Dutch oven and brown stew meat. Season meat with salt and pepper as you brown. When meat is browned, set aside.

Add onions, garlic, and balsamic vinegar to the Dutch oven. Cook 5 minutes and stir, scraping browned bits from the bottom of the Dutch oven as you stir.

Add tomato paste and return beef (and its juices) to the pot. Sprinkle with flour and stir.

Layer potatoes, celery and carrots on top of the stew meat. Then add all remaining ingredients to the Dutch oven.

Put lid on Dutch oven and place it inside the oven to cook. Cook for 5 hours. No peeking!

The secret to this recipe is to let it cook and not to peek.

SERVINGS	TIME	DELICIOUSNESS
8	330 *mins*	10

Inspired by Judy Murphy

One Pan Pizza

INGREDIENTS

- 2 Cups Bisquick
- 2 Eggs
- 2/3 Cup Milk
- 2 Cups Shredded Mozzarella
- 2 Tablespoons Italian Seasoning
- 4 Teaspoons Garlic Powder
- Sliced Pepperoni
- Sliced Salami
- 1/2 Cup Chopped White Onion
- 1 Diced Green Pepper
- 1 Can Whole Tomatoes
- 1/2 Cup Red Cooking Wine
- 1 Pack Chopped Fresh Basil
- 1 Tablespoon White Sugar
- 2 Tablespoons Olive Oil
- Salt & Pepper to Taste

DIRECTIONS

Preheat oven to 375 degrees. Grease rectangular baking dish.

Mix Bisquick, milk and eggs in a bowl. Batter will be lumpy. Stir into batter the pepperoni, salami, onions, green pepper, 1 tablespoon Italian seasoning, 2 teaspoons garlic powder, and 1 cup of mozzarella cheese.

Pour into baking dish and spread evenly.

Separately, pour whole tomatoes into a pot. With your hands, tear and crush the tomatoes to create a lumpy sauce. Add red cooking wine, fresh basil, sugar, olive oil, 1 tablespoon Italian seasoning, 2 teaspoons garlic powder and salt and pepper. Bring to boil, then lower heat to simmer for 10 minutes.

While sauce simmers, put baking dish in oven and bake until top is light brown (about 30 minutes).

Remove from oven and spread sauce over the top in desired amount. Top with remaining mozzarella cheese. Return to oven and bake until cheese is melted.

SERVINGS	TIME	DELICIOUSNESS
6	60 mins	10

Inspired by Pat Lucio

Potato Skins Fully Loaded

INGREDIENTS

- 4 Large Russet Potatoes
- 2 Cups Crumbled Bacon
- 2 Tablespoons Chopped Dill
- 2 Cups Shredded Sharp Cheddar Cheese
- 1 Bunch Chopped Scallions
- 1 Bunch Chopped Chives
- 1/2 Cup Green Pepper (Chopped)
- 1/2 Cup Red Pepper (Chopped)
- 1 Cup Sour Cream
- 2 Tablespoons Montreal Steak Seasoning
- Olive Oil
- Salt & Pepper to Taste

DIRECTIONS

Preheat oven to 400 degrees.

Rub potatoes in olive oil. Bake on foil-lined baking sheet for one hour or until skins are crisp. Remove and let cool for 10 minutes.

While cooling, slice uncooked bacon into tiny pieces and cook on stove. Remove crispy bacon pieces and reserve the grease.

Chop dill, scallions, chives, and peppers and mix together. Set aside.

Cut potatoes lengthwise to make wedges and hollow out the centers. Leave a 1/4 inch rim within the hollowed-out skin.

Lightly brush thin layer of bacon grease onto the interior of the potato skins. Top with cheddar cheese and bacon. Return to oven and set to broil. Cook until cheese melts.

Remove from oven. Season with salt, pepper and steak seasoning. Top with dill, scallion, chive and pepper mixture. Sprinkle on any remaining bacon and cheese.

Serve with scoop of sour cream.

SERVINGS	TIME	DELICIOUSNESS
8	90 mins	10

Inspired by Mary Rigg

Ramen Noodle Salad

INGREDIENTS

FOR THE DRESSING:

- 1/2 Cup Rice Wine Vinegar
- 3/4 Olive Oil
- 1/4 Cup White Cooking Wine
- 2 Packets of Chicken Flavored Top Ramen Seasoning
- Salt and Pepper (To Taste)

FOR THE SALAD

- 2 Cups Chopped Red Cabbage
- 1/2 Cup Chopped Green Onions
- 1/2 Cup Thinly Sliced Raddish
- 1/2 Cup Slivered Almonds
- 1/2 Cup Pumpkin Seeds
- 1 1/2 Cup Chopped Snap Peas
- 2 Packages of Ramen Noodles (Uncooked & Crumbled)

DIRECTIONS

For the dressing, mix all the ingredients together. Refrigerate overnight to allow the ingredients to marinate.

The salad itself can be mixed together the night before, but do not mix the salad and the dressing until ready to serve.

When you are ready to serve, toss dressing with salad and plate.

Enjoy!

SERVINGS	TIME	DELICIOUSNESS
2	IO mins	IO

Stefani Miller

Sour Cream Salsa

INGREDIENTS

- 16 Ounces Sour Cream
- 4 Tomatoes (Chopped)
- 1 Onion (Chopped)
- 1/4 Cup Fresh Dill (Chopped)
- 1/2 Cup Parsley (Chopped)
- 1/2 Cup Cilantro (Chopped)
- 4 Cloves Garlic (Minced)
- Juice of 1 Lime
- Salt & Pepper
- 1 Cup Shredded Mexican Cheese

DIRECTIONS

Chop all vegetables and mix together (I recommend you remove the gooey tomato seeds and discard). Adjust proportions as desired. Add lime juice. Salt and pepper to taste.

Add sour cream and cheese and stir to combine.

Serve with tortilla chips.

SERVINGS	TIME	DELICIOUSNESS
4	20 mins	10

Inspired by Frieda Easley

Spanish Cornbread

INGREDIENTS

- 2 Cups Cornmeal
- 2 Cups Flour
- 1 Teaspoon Baking Powder
- 2 Teaspoons Salt
- 1 Teaspoon Garlic Salt
- 1/2 Cup Sugar
- 3 Eggs
- 2 Cups Milk
- 1 Cup Sour Cream
- 1 Cup Jalapeno Peppers (Diced)
- 1 Yellow Onion
- 2 Ears Yellow Corn on the Cob
- 1/2 Cup Monterrey Jack Cheese
- 1/2 Cup Sharp Cheddar Cheese

DIRECTIONS

Preheat oven to 425 degrees. Preheat grill to medium high heat.

Peel back husks of corn, leaving the husks but allowing you to remove the hair. Then smooth husks back over the corn and soak in cold water for ten minutes.

Place corn on grill and cook for roughly 10 minutes. Remove corn, let cool. Then remove husks and slice the corn off the cob and set aside.

Chop onion and Jalapeno peppers.

Beat together eggs, sugar, garlic, milk, and sour cream. Then add peppers, onion, the corn from the cob, and both cheeses.

In a separate bowl, mix cornmeal, flour, baking powder and salt. Then slowly add dry ingredients to the wet ingredients until incorporated.

Pour batter into iron skillet and bake in oven for roughly one hour.

SERVINGS	TIME	DELICIOUSNESS
6	90 mins	10

Inspired by Keith Messer

Strawberry Salad

INGREDIENTS

FOR THE SALAD:
- 3 Ounces Slivered Almonds
- 2 Teaspoons Melted Butter
- 1 Teaspoon Sugar
- 1 Container Mixed Salad Greens
- 1 Cup Chopped Scallions
- 12 Strawberries
- 1 Cup Feta Cheese
- 1 Cup Bacon Bits

FOR THE DRESSING:
- 1/3 Cup Red Wine Vinegar
- 1 Minced Garlic Clove
- 1/3 Cup Olive Oil
- 1/3 Cup Sugar
- Salt and Pepper

DIRECTIONS

Combine ingredients for dressing in mason jar. Shake until thoroughly mixed. Set aside.

Preheat oven to 350 degrees. Arrange slivered almonds on greased cookie sheet. Drizzle almonds with melted butter and sprinkle with sugar. Toast until lightly browned, roughly eight to ten minutes.

Remove almonds from oven and set aside.

Remove stems from strawberries and slice into fourths.

In a large bowl, combine salad greens, feta cheese, bacon bits and strawberries. Add slivered almonds and toss until mixed.

Serve with dressing. Salt and pepper to taste.

SERVINGS 4

TIME 20 mins

DELICIOUSNESS 10

Heidi Ildhuso

Street Corn Grilled Cheese

INGREDIENTS

- 2 Ears Corn on the Cob (Grilled)
- 4 Tablespoons Butter
- 2 Tablespoons Fresh Chopped Cilantro
- 1 Teaspoon Grated Lime Zest
- Kosher Salt
- 4 Slices Sourdough Bread
- 6 Oz Grated Sharp Cheddar Cheese
- 2 Green Onions (Thinly Sliced)
- 2 Tablespoons Crumbled Cojita Cheese
- 1 Pinch Chili Lime Seasoning

DIRECTIONS

Turn the grill to high heat. Place corn directly on grill and cook until charred. Allow to cool and slice corn off the cob.

Stir together softened butter, cilantro, lime zest, and pinch of salt until combined.

Spread outside of the bread with cilantro lime butter. Heat a large skillet and place 2 slices of bread butter-side down. Top with cheese, corn and green onions. Top with the remaining slices of bread (butter side up).

Cook over low to medium heat. Go slow so the cheese melts. When bottom slice of bread is golden brown, flip and cook the other side.

Remove from heat. Top with cojita cheese, chili lime seasoning and cilantro.

Enjoy!

SERVINGS	TIME	DELICIOUSNESS
2	20 mins	10

Tatum Parker

Summer Street Corn

INGREDIENTS

- 4 Cobs of Fresh Corn
- Butter
- Paprika
- Salt & Pepper
- Cilantro (Finely Chopped)
- Cojita or Feta Cheese
- Lime

DIRECTIONS

Pull stalks on corn back but do not tear off. Remove as much of the "hair" as you can. Pull stalks back over the corn. Place corn in a large bowl of cold water and keep submerged for 15 minutes.

Turn on the grill until it reaches 400 degrees.

Remove corn from water and shake gently. Do not try to shake all the water loose. The water is necessary to cooking the corn. Place wet corn with stalks on the grill and cook for 10 minutes. Be sure to turn the corn so the stalks don't catch fire.

Remove corn from grill. Let cool 5 minutes. Then remove the stalks.

Lather corn in butter as desired. Then top with paprika, salt & pepper, cilantro and cheese. Squeeze generous amount of lime over corn.

Serve while warm.

You can change out cheese to suit your personal preference.

SERVINGS	TIME	DELICIOUSNESS
4	45 mins	10

INGREDIENTS

- 4 Avocados (Halved)
- 8 Slices Bacon (Crumbled)
- 1/2 Cup Butter
- 1/4 Cup Brown Sugar
- 1/4 Cup Ketchup
- 1/4 Cup Rice Wine Vinegar
- 1 Tablespoon Worcestershire

Inspired by Jeri Freimuth

Tangy Avocados & Bacon

DIRECTIONS

Cut avocados in half and remove pits. Set aside.

On stovetop, melt butter and add brown sugar, ketchup, rice wine vinegar, and Worcestershire. Simmer on stove and stir until sugar is dissolved and sauce has slightly reduced.

When ready to serve, drizzle sauce onto avocados. Then sprinkle with crispy bacon bits. Salt and pepper to taste.

SERVINGS	TIME	DELICIOUSNESS
4	20 mins	10

Ronald Earvin

Tomato Garlic Pasta

INGREDIENTS

- 1 Pound Bag of Pasta from Pasta Lago
- 3 Tablespoons Butter
- 10 Ounce Container of Cherry Tomatoes
- 6 Cloves Garlic
- 2 Cups White Cooking Wine
- 1 Cup Heavy Cream
- 1 Cup Parmesan Cheese
- 2 Tablespoons Corn Starch
- 1 Packet Fresh Basil
- 1 Lemon
- Salt & Pepper

DIRECTIONS

Slice tomatoes in half and chop basil. Set aside.

In a large pan, melt butter. Add minced garlic, stirring to prevent garlic from burning. Toss in tomatoes and stir until tomatoes begin to soften.

Add wine and bring to simmer. Add salt and pepper.

While sauce simmers, bring pot of water to boil and begin cooking pasta.

Allow sauce to cook out the alcohol. Then add heavy cream and stir to combine. Slowly add the cheese in portions, allowing cheese to melt and combine.

Sauce will be thin. Add water to the corn starch, stir, and then incorporate into the sauce until the sauce has thickened to a spaghetti sauce consistency.

Add basil. Drain noodles and add them to sauce. Stir to coat noodles.

Serve in dish. Sprinkle with pepper and add a generous squirt of fresh lemon juice on top.

SERVINGS	TIME	DELICIOUSNESS
4	30 mins	10

THE
INTERVIEWS

RESTAURANT INTERVIEWS

THE INTERVIEW PROCESS

In the following interviews, you'll get to hear from a wide variety of restaurant owners and chefs. Eight of these interviews were conducted as a group where our entire class met with the business owner. Often these were conducted on-site.

The remaining interviews were set up and executed by individual students who were required to identify a restaurant owner, track them down in any way possible, and interview them using our standard interview template.

For many students, this interview process was the most challenging of the entire cookbook project, as it required them to get far outside their comfort zone. What we learned throughout this interview process, however, was fascinating and informative.

For example, many restaurant owners and chefs in the Valley never intended to own a restaurant. Many hail from other fields: accounting, law, medicine, physical health, banking, etc. Almost every owner spoke about the challenges of running a business, the need to be a jack of all trades, and the incredible support of the local residents of the Valley.

For anyone who wants a peek behind the curtain and a deeper understanding of the culinary world currently at work in Chelan today, this section is for you.

This section also includes a wide array of photos taken all over Chelan. These photos are intentionally left unlabeled to inspire our readers to go and seek out the wonders and oddities that are in every nook and cranny of the Valley.

THE ALBATROSS

The Albatross

I met up with Kane, the head chef at The Alabtross, which is located in the same building as the Pro Shop at the Lake Chelan Municipal Golf Course. It was a sweltering day for mid-March, and we sat outside and tried to enjoy the sunshine.

The Albatross is one of the newest restaurants in Chelan. It opened in 2022 and has been improving each year.

I'm a golfer myself and have been to the Albatross many times. It was fascinating to learn more about the restaurant and the people cooking the food I'd eaten so many times before. It definitely made me appreciate the experience that much more.

Wyatt
How long have you worked for The Albatross?

Albatross
I was working for Julie about a month before we opened. So three years now.

Wyatt
And the Albatross opened when?

Albatross
In 2022.

Wyatt
What kind of food do you serve?

Albatross
We serve what's called Contemporary American food.

Wyatt
Why did you become a chef?

Albatross
I've always loved to cook. When I first got out of high school, I wasn't entirely sure I wanted to be a chef, but I eventually decided to go to culinary school. And I just fell in love with it. I like creating, being creative with food. I love eating, obviously.

Wyatt
What did you do before working as a chef?

Albatross

I was in school. Culinary school. My first job was at Lakeview Drive-In. I was 16. So I've been cooking since I was 16.

Wyatt

How did you decide to what kind of food to serve at the Landing?

Albatross

We pick food based on the feedback we get from customers. What food they like. What dishes they don't care for. We try to cater to our customers as much as we can.

With that in mind, we also select food based on what we feel like we can execute with quality and speed.

Wyatt

Where are you from originally?

Albatross

Originally? Gillette, Wyoming. But I moved around a lot growing up. I actually lived in Chelan for a while when I was a little kid. I went to MOE.

Wyatt

What do you like most about working at The Albatross?

Albatross

This is a great working environment. The owners are great. They want the whole staff to have fun. Julie really takes care of her staff. And this is a beautiful place. It's hard to complain about coming to work at a place like this.

Wyatt

What does a normal day look like for you?

Albatross

First thing, I come in and try to look at everything, make sure I have my prep list lined up. I'll start a prep list the night before, then finish it up in the morning. Then I turn everything on: the stove, the fryer. Then I prep. Once the prep's all done, we let the front of the house know if there are any specials for the day, give them the counts on things so they know if we're low on anything.

And then we open. So then I'm in the back cooking and helping with cleaning, keeping things in order. And then we clean up at the end of the night.

Wyatt

What were you most surprised by when you started working here?

Albatross

Well, this has been the most remote location I've worked at. Chelan doesn't necessarily seem remote, but compared to the city it's really different, right? We get deliveries twice a week here, that's it, rather than every day. There are limits on what you can get delivered here, that sort of thing.

Wyatt

How did you create your menu?

Albatross

When Julie hired me they already had a basic menu that they'd planned out. So I mostly just tweaked that to make it more efficient. And then each season we've tried to introduce new things while keeping the items people really enjoy.

If we have an item that's just not selling, then we may move on from it and try something new. So we try to keep it fresh and keep trying things to see what works.

Wyatt

What's your favorite item on the menu?

Albatross

The salmon piccata. That's a new one this season. It's really tasty.

Wyatt

My dad loves that one. He gets it every time we come here.

Albatross

That's probably my favorite. And the steak fillet. I love steak, and we have a very high quality fillet.

Wyatt

What do you like to cook at home?

Albatross

Well, it depends on what kind of mood I'm in. But I make a lot of mac and cheese for myself, a lot of ramen noodles. I'm actually working on a recipe for ramen noodles, something fresh with a broth from scratch, not those dried spice packets.

Wyatt

What do you like about being a chef in Chelan?

Albatross

It's close to my family. That's really great. And I love to cook. It's an art form, really, and working here I'm able to be creative and try new things with food. I also really enjoy being able to take a dish that people enjoy and find new ways to tweak it to introduce them to something that's just a little different and little more interesting and that maybe they'll like even more.

Wyatt
Did you always want to be a chef?

Albatross
Not necessarily. I knew I enjoyed cooking. And I loved being in the kitchen, even when I was a little kid. I helped my grandma in the kitchen a lot. But it wasn't really until I got to culinary school that I was certain this was what I wanted to do. I loved the energy of the kitchen, the excitement in there, working with the team.

Wyatt
Why should people come to the Albatross?

Albatross
I think we're one of the best new restaurants in Chelan. It's great food, a great location. Our whole team loves being here, and Julie takes good care of her staff. That kind of thing, it trickles down to the customers. Happy employees make for a better experience for the customer, right?

And we're always trying to do new things, so there's always something fresh and different. If people want a good experience with great food in a beautiful setting, then they should check us out.

APPLE BERRIES

Apple Berries Juice Bar

Apple Berries Juice Bar is located in the Chelan Plaza, the little strip mall that is also home to the Lake Chelan Bakery and All For Paws Pet Boutique. I met with Stephanie, the owner of Apple Berries, to talk about why she opened a juice bar here in Chelan, her inspirations, and how she feels about running a business in the Valley.

Apple Berries is one of the newest restaurants in town, having just opened their doors in 2022. But they are offering something unique and different from what can be found anywhere else in town.

Tiana

You opened just a few years ago, correct?

Apple Berries

I did. We opened in 2022.

Tiana

How many employees do you have?

Apple Berries

Just one. We're a pretty small operation.

Tiana

What kind of food do you serve?

Apple Berries

Gluten free, dairy free, sugar free. And that's no cane sugar. Any sugar in our smoothies or anything comes purely from the food itself, the natural sugars in the fruits or vegetables, the agave, honey or maple syrup. We don't add any cane sugar or brown sugar or anything like that.

Tiana

Why were you inspired to open a juice bar?

Apple Berries

Two reasons. First, I love it. I love fresh food. I love healthy food. I love smoothies. And second, I've always had digestion issues myself. My whole life it's been a challenge to find things that I can eat that don't upset my system. I always knew there were other people out there too, people who suffered from various digestion problems. So opening Apple Berries is partially about helping those people, providing food for people who struggle to find something that their bodies can be happy with.

Tiana

What did you do before you owned Apple Berries?

Apple Berries

I worked with my ex-husband before this. I dealt with insurance and lawyers and all that kind of stuff. A very different kind of experience from what I do here.

Tiana

Where are you from originally?

Apple Berries

California.

Tiana

What do you like most about owning a juice bar?

Apple Berries

The customer service. I love connecting with people. So many different people come through the door. I enjoy meeting people and connecting with them and helping them find something on the menu that they're going to enjoy.

Tiana

What does a normal day look like for you?

Apple Berries

Anxious. Busy and exciting.

Tiana

What kind of prep is involved with running a juice bar?

Apple Berries

Good question. We come in every day and first thing you make sure everything's stocked up. All the produce. Then Avery, the young lady who helps me, she starts all the baking. She'll bake for the day, or bake enough for a few days so we can freeze some of it.

That doesn't include salads, of course. Salads are fresh. They have a short shelf life, and you obviously can't freeze those.

So there's a fair amount of prep, and you prep, prep, prep, make, make, make, serve, serve, serve. Round and round.

Tiana

What were you most surprised by after opening?

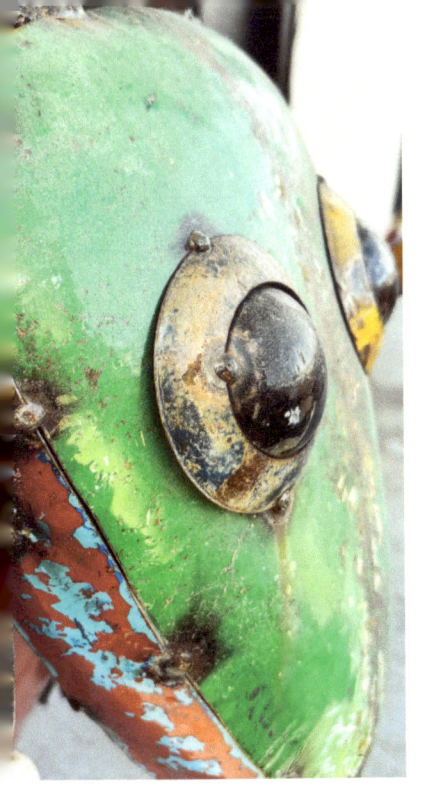

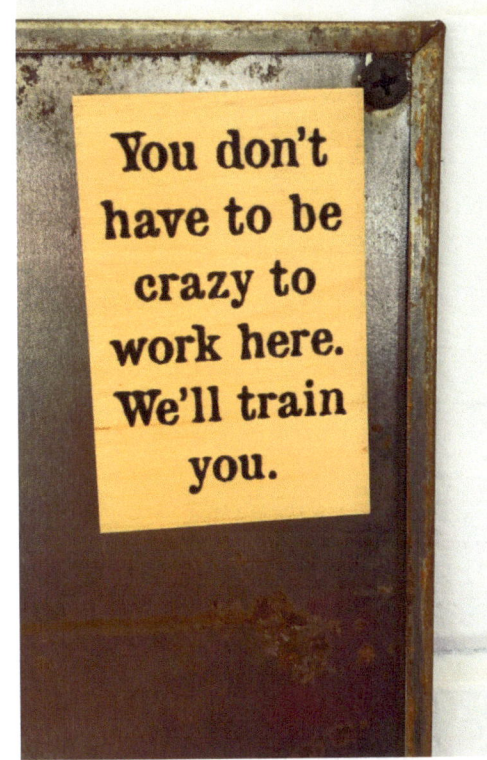

You don't
have to be
crazy to
work here.
We'll train
you.

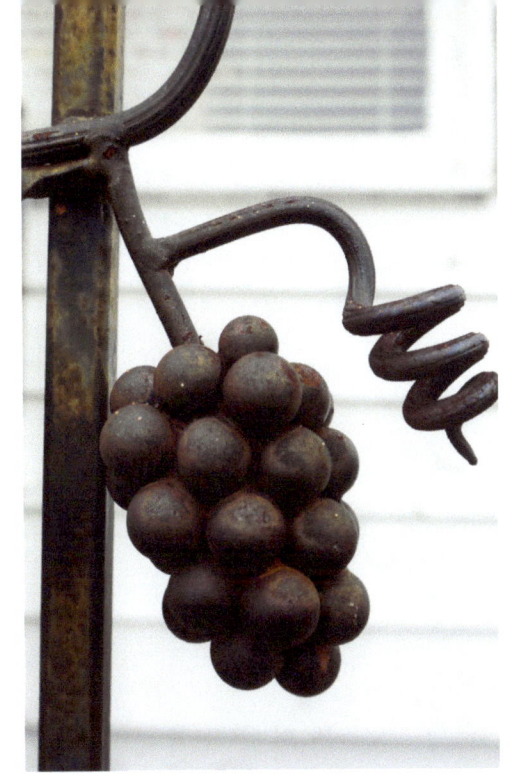

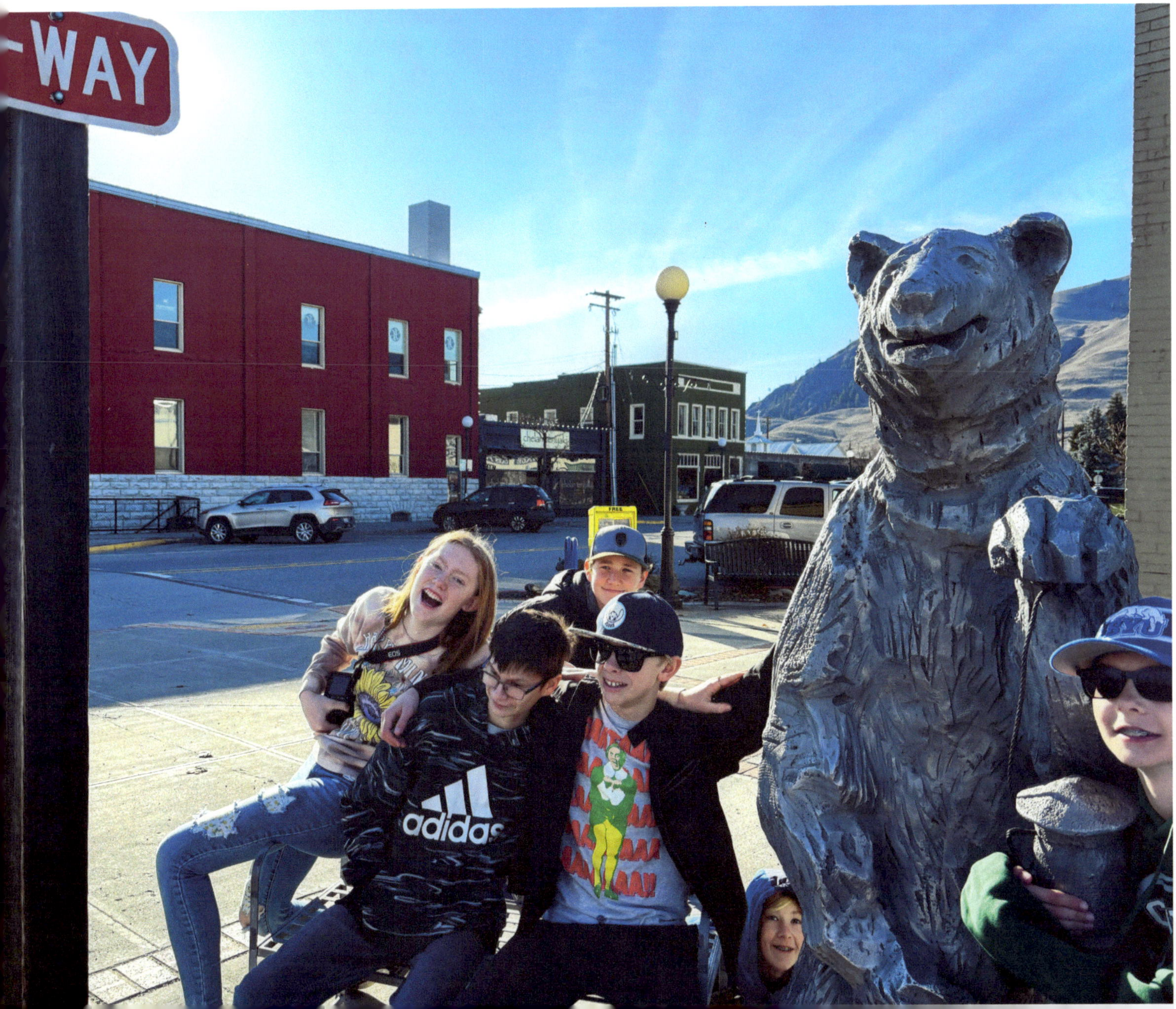
WAY
adidas

Apple Berries

How much people liked it. I mean I love it, but you never know if people will love it the way you do. We've been very lucky so far. People have really responded to what we're doing.

Tiana

What is your favorite item on the menu?

Apple Berries

Anything with chocolate.

Tiana

What is the hardest thing to make?

Apple Berries

The juices. There's a lot of prep work behind a juice. It takes a lot of effort. For example, our Number One on the menu. It's got kale, celery, apple, lemon, ginger, and cucumber. It takes six to eight minutes to make that, to get it together and press and then clean up. And then you have to clean the machine. It's not necessarily that complicated, but it's time consuming, especially when you've got a line out the door and people waiting.

Tiana

What do you like about owning a restaurant in Chelan?

Apple Berries

The customers. This is a very unique valley and the community is just very supportive.

Tiana

Did you always want to own a restaurant?

Apple Berries

No. I was going to open a retail store because I love clothing. I was going to open a clothing store and it just didn't work out. This did.

Tiana

Why should people go to your restaurant?

Apple Berries

It's a good alternative to junk food. And it tastes good and it's healthy. I'd say especially if you have any food issues, any digestive problems or anything like that, come on by.

APPLE CUP

Apple Cup Cafe

I met with Ryan Peterson, owner and operator of Apple Cup Cafe. Right off the bat he offered me a milkshake. It's hard not to like a guy who offers you a milkshake the first time you meet him. In addition to the interview itself, Ryan showed me around the kitchen and explained how they make their food and where they store everything.

"You want to shake some pots and pans?" he asked.

Why not? I shook the pots and pans and almost felt like a real chef.

The day after our interview, the Apple Cup experienced a terrible fire caused by an equipment failure. The back end of the cafe was severely damaged, including the collapse of the roof over a large section of the building, leading to the restaurant's closure until all the necessary repairs and renovations could be completed.

In the wake of the fire, the Apple Cup saw a tremendous outpouring of support from the community, making it clear that this beloved restaurant means a great deal to people throughout the valley.

Dean:
When did the Apple Cup open?

Apple Cup:
1957. It was originally called the Snack Shack, but the name was changed. The Apple Cup was the name of the hydroplane races that were held here in Chelan from 1957 to 1960.

Dean:
How many employees do you have?

Apple Cup:
About 30.

Dean:
What kind of food do you serve?

Apple Cup:
We do breakfast, lunch and dinner. It's really family style food. Generous portions. Comfort food. We like people to feel like they get a hearty meal at a good price.

Dean:
Why did you go into the restaurant business?

Apple Cup:

This was my family's restaurant. I was eight when my parent's bought it. So I've been running around here since I was eight years old.

Dean:

What did you do before this?

Apple Cup:

I was in the medical field. Not very exciting. It was an administrative job. I was an Intake Director. What I did is known as Utilization Review. Basically, I argued with insurance companies all day. Like I said: not very exciting.

Dean:

How did you decide upon the type of food you serve?

Apple Cup:

Well, partially because I love breakfast food. I love pancakes, hash browns, eggs, that sort of thing. So the menu reflects a lot of what I enjoy eating. But mostly we've always tried to provide food that feels like quality American home cooking.

Dean:

Where are you from originally?

Apple Cup:

I was born in Atlanta, but Chelan is really the only home I've known. I don't remember anything before moving here as a kid.

Dean:

What's a normal day look like for you?

Apple Cup:

It's a lot of going around and making sure the customers are happy. Then there's the administrative stuff, counting tills, doing reports, that kind of thing. If we're not too busy, I'm forecasting, trying to come up with new marketing ideas, testing recipes.

There's obviously a lot of managing people. With 30 employees, there's a fair amount of managing people that takes place.

Dean:

What surprised you the most about owning a restaurant?

Apple Cup:

Just how difficult it can be to manage so many people. It's a large staff, so there are just so many things that can come up. You've got 30 different lives intersecting with yours, and so it's a lot to keep track of and work with. We've got a great staff.

VISIBLE REGISTER
0000

ABRAHAM LINCOLN

and

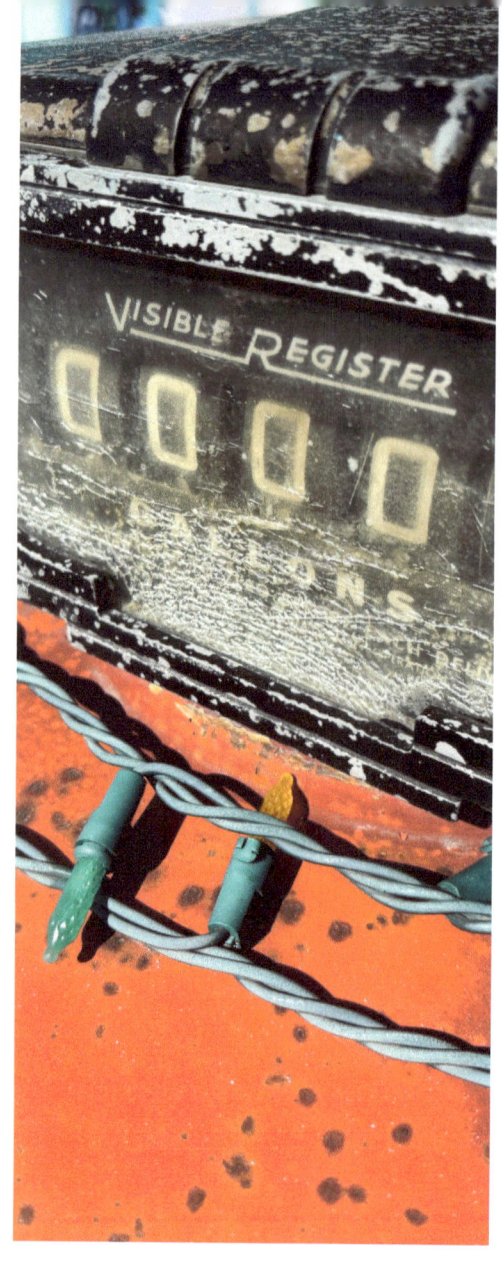

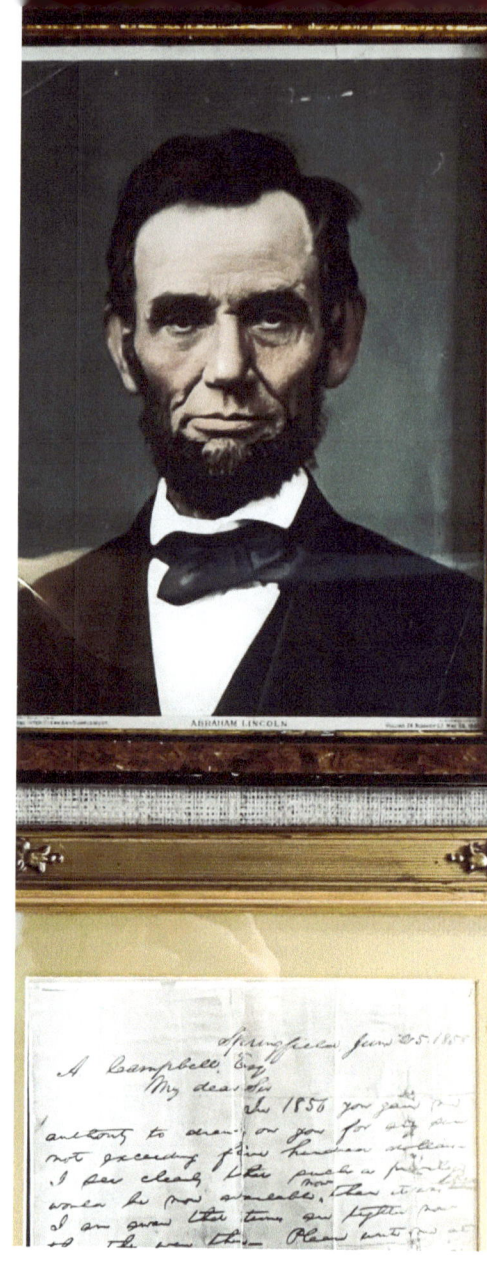

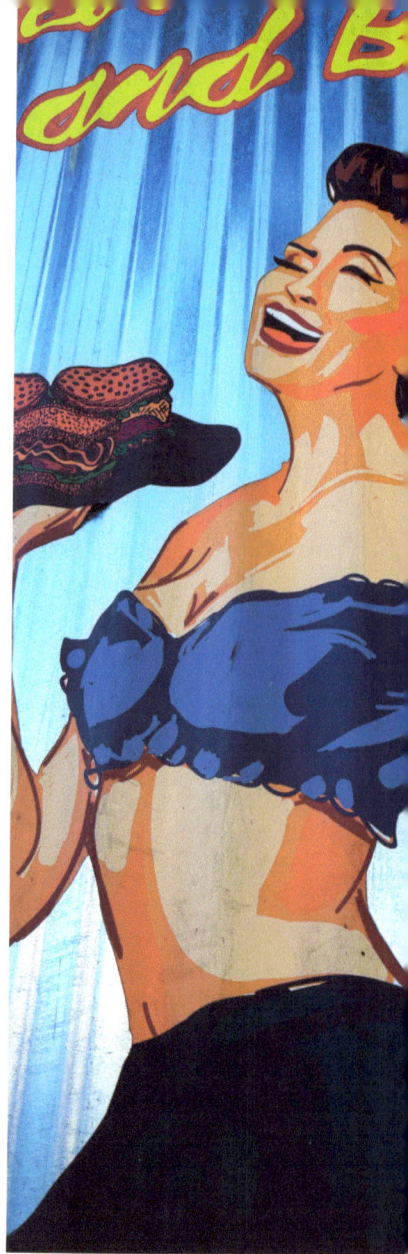

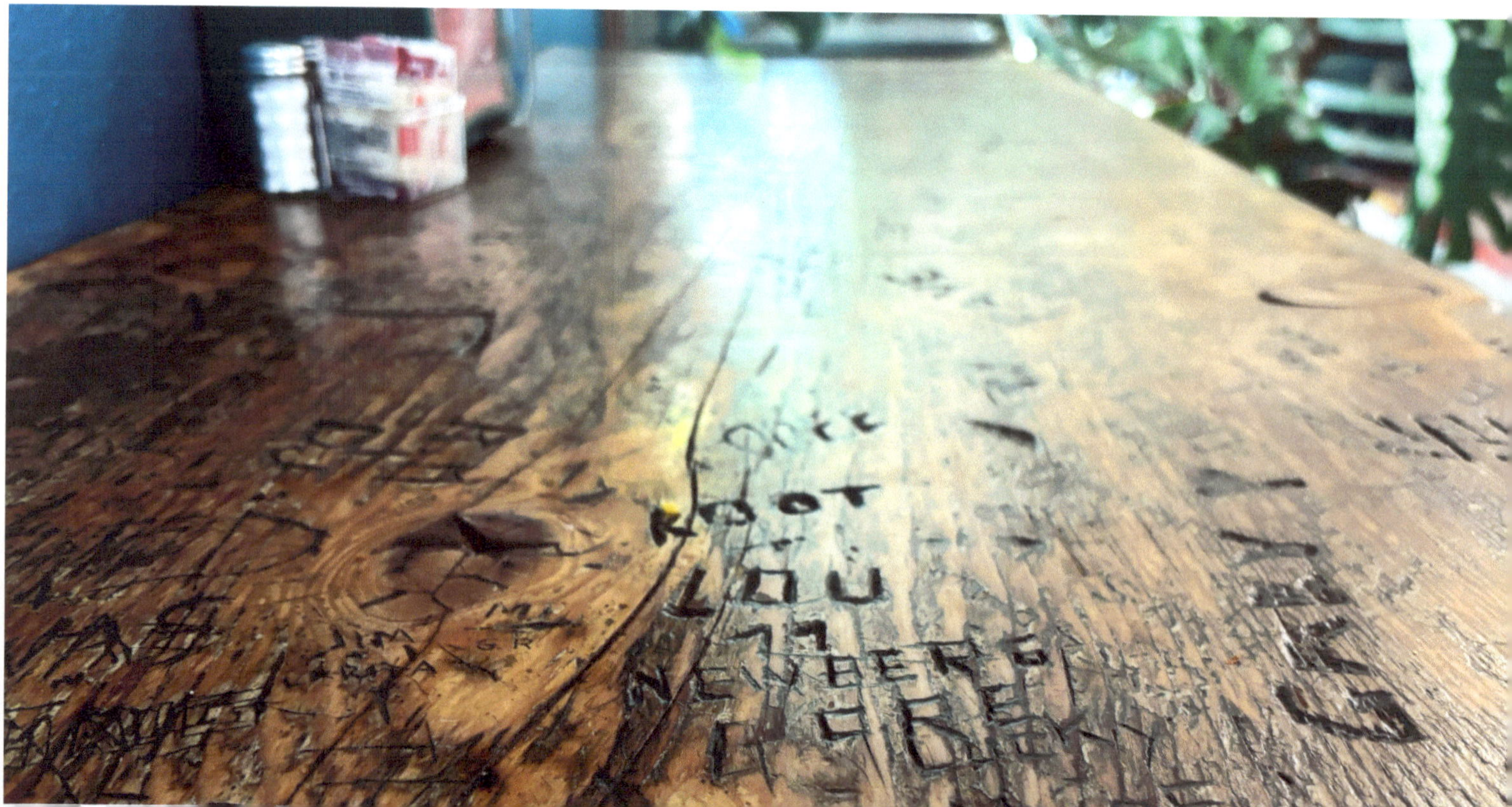
KOOT
LOU
NEWBERG

Dean:
What's your role specifically?

Apple Cup:
These days it's mostly administrative. I don't do much of the day to day stuff anymore.

Dean:
What do you like most about running a restaurant in Chelan?

Apple Cup:
Meeting people. I love talking to different people. In the restaurant business, you just get to meet so many different kinds of people.

Dean:
How did your family come to own the Apple Cup?

Apple Cup:
My mom had purchased the business from a man named Mr. Keller. She ran it for about 18 years, and then I bought it from her.

Dean:
Why should people come to the Apple Cup?

Apple Cup:
They should come for breakfast and see what we're all about. I'd say people should come because we offer good food, decent prices, good service, and we can get you in and out pretty dang quick.

BLUEBERRY HILLS

Blueberry Hills

"We tried everything."

Kari Sorensen, owner and operator of Blueberry Hills in Manson, is recounting their struggles with their famous blueberry pies after their usual corn starch manufacturer altered their product. To the degree that the average person thinks about corn starch, they probably don't imagine it to be a product all that difficult to replace. They'd be wrong.

In this case, the proper starch was the difference between pies that properly set up and were good for eating and a soupy mess of cooked blueberries.

Roots
What happened to the original corn starch you were using?

Kari
They don't make it anymore. National is the brand name, and they're out of California, but my supplier was Spokane Bakery Supply. At one point during COVID the SBS quit carrying it. Then I had to go find it again.

National sent me about a hundred samples of corn starches. They have hundreds. They even make starch for cardboard boxes to make them harder. I'm like, no, I'm looking for pie, not cardboard. Pie. I don't want it that stiff.

Eventually we found it and they had changed the name. They were willing to sell us a truckload. Well, during COVID, we didn't have any money to buy a truckload. And now they've cut down to only two people working in distribution, and they can't fulfill us.

And the Bakery Supply changed hands. Now they're Bakemark. I can't get them to carry it again because we're the only customer that wants it.

Our conversation turns from the difficulties of tracking down the proper starch to how Blueberry Hills fared during the COVID pandemic.

Kari
We had all the doors open, and we took orders outside. We moved all the tables out into the parking lot. We set up a barbecue spit made out of a 1954 Chevy flatbed truck. We did Hawaiian barbecue out there. We were able to kind of open inside, we had all the doors open. We had fans going. I mean, this is in the winter.

And we have the air quality monitors. We have the temperature sensors. We have, we did everything that they asked us to do.

Roots

You guys have seen a lot of success out here.

Kari

Our success is actually the thing that hurts us. You know, people wait in line for an hour and a half in the summer, and then they wait almost two hours for their food to arrive sometimes. But we always tell people how long the wait is going to be.

Roots

Has this property always been in your family?

Kari

It's been in my family's since the early 1900s. I'm actually fifth generation. And Blueberry Hills was built back in 2000.

Mom and dad were full-time apple farmers. Here we thought we were just building a little fruit stand. This property was full of apples, but the apples didn't make money anymore.

We had friends that were actually the first commercial blueberry growers down in Arkansas: Ed and Barb Brown. They propagated the plants and started a U-pick. This is the 1960s and nobody's heard of blueberries before. They knew huckleberries but not blueberries.

People came from all over the Midwest to pick blueberries but people were like: what do we do with them? Eat them? Cook them? So they bought a little waffle iron and built a cracker shack. I've seen pictures. It was a dump is what it was, walls that barely stood up, but it's what they had, and they made do with what they had. They started cooking in it and making blueberry pie filling and put that on top of the waffles. And people understood that. They understood waffles and pie filling.

They did great. Great business. A huge success for about ten years, and then they had a really bad drought. They didn't have irrigation like we do today. The drought killed all the plants and they lost the farm and moved to Bellingham. And my mom and dad knew them, and when they wanted to plant blueberries, they called up Ed and asked what he thought about growing blueberries in Chelan.

We talked to all the experts on local farming, the folks from WSU, the fertilizer places and the co-ops and the other farmers and field men, and everybody told us: don't do it. Blueberries won't grow out here. You're wasting your money. But Dad went ahead and did it and they've grown great.

Roots

When did you open your doors?

Kari

We opened in November of 2002. The only thing we had on our menu was blintzes, which are large sweet crepes filled with ricotta and cream cheese. We would do peach and blueberry pie filling on those. And we had Danish waffles. Or you could have a hamburger. That's it.

People always say: you must be restaurant people. You've done so well. And Dad likes to say: yea, we've eaten in a lot of restaurants.

Roots

How long did it take to grow the blueberry plants?

Kari

We put them in the ground the first year. But there were very few blueberries on the plants that first year. We had 13,000 plants. Second year they doubled in size but there weren't enough to pick. Then we opened the third year.

So we're waiting for those blueberries to ripen, and every day we'd go out and look. But they're not ready, they're not ready. We didn't even know what they were supposed to look like when they were ripe, but we'd eat them and taste test. And finally the day comes, we know they're ripe and tomorrow's gonna be the day we can pick these big beautiful blueberries.

And we go out the next morning and there's not one blueberry in the entire field. The birds had been waiting just like us, and the birds got every single one of them.

Roots

How did you deal with the birds?

Kari

Kestrels. Kestrels are the world's smallest falcon. We put up kestrel nests. They patrol within half a mile of their nest and dive bomb the other birds.

Roots

How many blueberries do you pick per year?

Kari

It works out to about three to four hundred thousand pounds each year. We individually quick freeze all the blueberries we pick and put them in our freezer. Or we sell them fresh at the fruit stand. We also sell them in five pound bags to Cisco Foods and wholesalers in Montana, Oregon, Idaho, all over the Pacific Northwest.

Roots

How did it go that first year?

Kari

Crazy. We didn't know anything. I mean, do we use paper plates? Dishes? Mom wanted to do pies, but she also wanted to do empanadas, which are deep fried. So we needed a deep fryer, and then the health department said we had to have a hood in case of a grease fire. And Dad says: well, if we're gonna have a deep fryer, why not a flat top too? And why not burners where we can do eggs. So eggs went on the menu.

It just took on a life of its own. And then we were discovered by Go Magazine. We had no idea they were doing an article. One Saturday we came to work and there was a line all the way to the road, and we didn't know what to do. We were panicked.

And of course the neighbors were mad because we were just supposed to be a little fruit stand and now there were lines of people out in the road.

Roots

What do you think is the key to running a successful restaurant in a small town?

Kari

Committing to the locals and being consistent. We're going to be here from eight in the morning to three in the afternoon without fail, even if we have a slow day. People can count on us. And we want to promise people that the drive out here is worth it.

Roots

How have you handled the changes in the economy over the last few years?

Kari

It's been rough. The cost of food is astronomic. Everything has gone up: electricity, gas, property taxes, salaries, the cost of food has doubled. But I can't just say well now my burger that used to be $15 is now $30. People won't pay that.

There's lots of ways restaurants can make money when the economy is rough, and one way is to lower quality. And we didn't want to do that. We actually have increased the quality of our food. I'm really picky about the quality of our food.

Right now, we're looking at four different types of flour. We're experimenting, because we've noticed the new flour we've been getting isn't as good. It's grittier, not as fine. Doesn't feel as good in your mouth. And so we're looking at other flours.

Roots

Can we come back and pick blueberries sometime?

Kari

Come on back around Labor Day. I'm on the radio, on KOZI. Blueberry Kari they call me. Listen on the radio because we'll announce when the blueberries are ripe and ready. We'd love to have you back.

BROKEN COMPASS

Broken Compass Cafe

I met Willow Brown and her mother, the owners of the Broken Compass Cafe at Riverwalk Inn, on a Thursday afternoon. I spoke with them about how they came to be here in Chelan and how they left the medical field to go into the hospitality and restaurant business. Our class has made many trips to the Broken Compass over the course of the year and discovered that their baked goods -- especially their cinnamon rolls -- are not to be missed. Willow was kind enough to share with us her phenomenal blueberry scone recipe, which she says many people have asked for and which she has never (until now) given to anybody.

Thank you, Willow!

Ethan

You guys opened in 2023, is that right?

Willow

Yep. Last year on Mother's Day.

Ethan

Why did you want to open a restaurant?

Willow

It's been my mom's dream for a long time. She's wanted to own a restaurant since she was a kiddo. Took her until 54, but we finally got it.

Ethan

What did you guys do before this?

Willow

We were both in the medical field. I was a phlebotomist, which means I drew a lot of blood. Mom was a kidney dialysis specialist. She did the more important stuff.

Ethan

That's a totally different field.

Willow

Yeah, we were super busy all the time. It's a lot harder mentally to be in the medical field, but here with the cafe it's harder physically. So they're different, but they're both difficult in their own way.

Ethan

You guys specialize in breakfast, correct?

Willow:

We do. Everybody needs breakfast, right? Not everybody necessarily wants dinner, and maybe not everybody wants lunch. But everybody wants breakfast. That was the idea, and so far it's worked out pretty well.

Ethan

Where are you from originally?

Willow:

Alaska.

Ethan:

What do you like most about owning a restaurant?

Willow:

Being my own boss. Besides my mom, I don't have anyone telling me what to do. So I get to create the rules. We got to create our own menu, our own coffee. I try to be a good boss and not yell at people or tell people what to do all day. We have a great staff that knows what they're doing.

Ethan:

What's a normal day look like for you?

Willow:

We usually start about 4:00 in the morning. We get here pretty early. We prep all the baked goods, and breakfast service starts at 8:00. Which means we're prepping the kitchen at 7:00. We get everything cut up, sorted and organized. Then you've got your day, and at the end you gotta clean everything up. Then you come back the next morning. It's like a merry-go-round. You do the same basic things each day.

Ethan:

What surprised you most about running a restaurant?

Willow:

Probably how much people like the food. It was scary because we'd curated the menu and decided everything. What went into things, what seasonings, everything. And we thought people might hate it. You never know. But people really like the food.

Ethan:

How'd you craft the menu?

Willow:

We sat down and thought: what would we eat? You know, what would we make for dinner? What would we want for lunch? We didn't really think about what other people would want necessarily. We started with ourselves. What would we want to eat for breakfast? And then we worked from there. Everything on the menu is something we've made at home ourselves. Nothing is a recipe we found online or anything like that. It's just food we've made and food we love.

Ethan:
What's your favorite item on the menu?

Willow:
The sticky bun is my favorite. We make a homemade caramel for that. Fresh pecans in there. I like it more than the cinnamon roll, which says a lot.

Ethan:
What's the hardest thing to make?

Willow:
The sticky bun. You start with a cinnamon roll base, and then the fresh caramel. You have to cover them perfectly. The pecan ration has to be just right. And they take an hour in the oven. Cinnamon rolls are much easier.

Ethan:
What do you like about owning a business here in Chelan?

Willow:
I love the people. Locals and tourists both. I've always been a people person. I love meeting all these people from different states, different countries and provinces, wherever they may be from. I love all the different personalities.

Ethan:
Did you always want to own a restaurant?

Willow:
I always wanted to own a cafe. I always wanted to do coffee. Not so much the cooking part, but I've learned how to do that too. Great skill to learn. To be able to feed people food you've created by hand is huge, a big ego booster.

Ethan:
Why should people come to Riverwalk Inn?

Willow:
We make great food. It's always fresh. It's always homemade. We pick all our produce and products by hand. Everything is ripe and fresh. If you want really tasty baked goods that are made by hand, then give us a shot and see what you think.

CAMPBELL'S PUB

Campbell's Pub

Tom and Eric Campbell came to Roots to give a presentation on the history of their resort and how it developed from a small hotel into a thriving lakefront destination. Few businesses – in Chelan or anywhere else – have stayed in continuous operation for over a hundred years. Few of those have also remained within the hands of the original family that first opened the doors. Campbell's has.

Tom

Our great, great grandfather, CC Campbell came over from Sioux City in the late 1800s. This was like the wild west out here. Cowboys, pioneers. He was a judge and a lawman in charge of a dry parish, so he wasn't exactly the most popular guy around.

Eric

I think he may have honestly feared for his family's safety. So he made his way west. He went by himself at first from Sioux City. Hopped on a train and came out west.

Tom

He ended up in Wilbur, Washington. He walked from Wilbur to Chelan.

Eric

It took him four days. He walked the whole way by himself. And he got to Chelan and saw the lake, and I think he just fell in love with the valley right off the bat.

Roots

Did he always intend to come to Chelan?

Tom

He was on a solo mission, but I think he knew some people in the area, which is how he heard of it in the first place.

Our conversation turns to the early layout of Chelan. Tom and Eric have brought photos of the early days of the hotel that will eventually become the centerpiece of Campbell's Resort.

Roots

What kind of people were coming to the Hotel back then?

Tom

Well, there was a lot of mining up lake. Folks were coming to Chelan to get rich. There were prospectors, and of course prostitutes. Everyone's out there trying to strike gold.

Eric

So CC built the old hotel with 16 rooms. He moved his family over, his son and his wife. His wife was known as a great cook. And they basically took care of all these people coming through town. They'd stay at the hotel, get a good meal, and head up lake.

Tom

It was pretty humble beginnings. They had a very lean crew. Tourism didn't exist back then. Not here. People didn't put their families in the horse and carriage and come to Chelan for vacation. This was workers, mostly men, people trying to get out and make money to take back. It wasn't people having a good time. The traveling for vacation didn't really start until the 50s.

Roots

Your great, great grandfather had a son, correct?

Tom

Yes. Arthur. He was an infant. He later went to the University of Washington. He was on the original crew team.

Eric

You've heard of *The Boys in the Boat*? Arthur was about 15 years before that. He was on the first UW rowing team. They went to Poughkeepsie to compete in the national championship. That team really put the UW rowing team on the map.

Tom

They placed third, but they only lost by a length. It was a big deal because people didn't really take Western rowing teams seriously. And now UW has 19 national championships. They're second all-time behind just Cornell.

Roots

Did either of you row in college?

Eric

We did. I rowed for three years, and Tom rowed too. It's a lot of work, but it's a lot of fun too. If you go to college and have the opportunity to row, we highly recommend it.

Tom

Arthur was also one of the first graduating classes in Chelan. Class of 1908. There were four people that graduated that year from Chelan. After that he was a banker in Illinois for a short time. Then he moved back to Chelan and met his wife. She was a schoolteacher. There's a crazy story about him actually.

The story is he came back one summer when he was at UW. He was supposed to be incredibly strong. Just strong as an ox.

Eric

I believe there was an article about him that claimed he was the strongest man at the University of Washington campus. That he did 100-pound dumbbell curls, that kind of thing.

Tom

So the story is that he dug out the entire downstairs dining room by himself. If you've been to the restaurant, we have the dining room downstairs. The whole building is constructed on a sandbar, and the story is he dug out that entire space one summer. All by himself. Just a shovel and a wheelbarrow.

Roots

How did Campbell's fare during the Depression?

Eric

Our grandfather, he wrote some memoirs before he passed. He wrote about his experiences in the 20s and the Depression. The whole family came back during the Depression. They lived at the resort and worked there.

Tom

The family was orchardists and they had to sell a ton of orchard land to get through those years. All the family pitched in. It was just a different world. And then World War II happened, and our Uncle Dan, he was an Army pilot. He flew in the Aluetian Islands.

Eric

And our grandfather was a radio technician for the Army, but he didn't have any combat experiences. Both of them came back though, and they worked together to build the business. It's the 1950s then, and Chelan was starting to become known as a vacation destination.

When you look at Campbell's, you can see all the motel-looking buildings. That's from the 50s. You could drive your car right up to the door and walk right in. It was called the Highway Motorport. That was really the start of recreational tourism.

Tom

And now we have families, they've been coming here every summer since the 50s or 60s or 70s. Year after year. That's what Art and Dan did. That's what they established. They built these motel buildings and laid the foundation for everything we do now.

Roots

Where did you two start in the business?

Eric

We worked in the business growing up just like Dad and our grandfather. We washed dishes, bussed tables, delivered newspapers, whatever. You name it. We did all of it.

Roots

Where do most of your guests come from?

Eric

About 85% of our guests come from the Puget Sound.

Roots

How many people do you employ?

Eric

In the summer, we employ about 250 people. Off season, that drops to about 150.

Roots

And how many guests?

Tom

We host over 60,000 guests every year.

Roots

Are you guys involved in the tourism industry outside of just Campbell's?

Tom

Eric and I are pretty involved. You have to be involved, right? You have to have a seat at the table. That's one thing that's always been important to us. You have to have a seat at the table and talk about the things that are going on.

Eric's been involved in the Hospitality Association, which is statewide. I've been in with the Tourism Alliance at the state level. Eric's been a part of the Historic Downtown Association. We've both been President of the Chamber of Commerce. We're even active in the Wenatchee Chamber.

Eric

If it's related to tourism or touches our community, I think that's something we want to be involved with. We want to be able to contribute and do our part and support the valley and the community and everyone who lives here.

Tom

And it's not just tourism. For example, we support Phil Long's Lake Chelan Research Institute. We contribute to that. Anything we can do to maintain water quality is really important. Without our natural ecosystem, we've got nothing, right?

Roots

What really separates Campbell's from everyone else?

Eric

Obviously the history is unique. This is our 123rd year. That's pretty special. We started in 1901, same year as Nordstrom. You know the founder of Nordstrom went up to the Yukon Gold Rush and actually was lucky enough to find some gold and brought it back to open a shoe store in downtown Seattle. And we started the same year.

Tom

And Campbell's is still in the same family. Five generations and 123 years later, we're still here. We're still working it every day. If you want to find us, you know where we're at. Our dad still works. Forty-six years he's been working here. Even our grandfather, before he passed away, he worked basically until the end.

Eric

He'd come in – this is when he was really old and couldn't do much anymore – but he'd come in and talk with us. He'd count lounge furniture. He'd walk around and check on things. He did it until he just couldn't physically do it anymore. Our whole family has been like that. Boots on the ground, and you always work. No excuses.

Tom

We're really lucky. I mean, we have 250 people, right? That's every day in the summer. That's 250 lives, and we're on 24 hours a day. Our front desk is always open. Seven days a week. So you try to surround yourself with awesome people. We're really lucky to have so many cool people that work with us. It's a team. It's 100% a team effort.

Eric

Honestly, we wouldn't be here right now if it wasn't for our staff and all the people who've come before us. We're standing on the shoulders of all those people: our dad and our grandfather and everyone. They started it. They had it and built it. We're just honoring their legacy.

Tom

And hopefully we'll leave it in a better place than when we first found it.

Roots

Did you always want to work in this industry?

Tom

No. I'd say after high school, I just wanted to get out of here. But there's something about Chelan. It calls you back. There's a magic to it. Something about the lake and the community.

I was always interested in cooking. I cooked a lot with my grandmother. I think I probably frustrated Mom in the kitchen quite a bit. So I was interested, but it wasn't exactly what I thought I'd be doing when I got older.

Eric

Same. Eventually we both came back, and now I get to work with my brother, who I really enjoy.

Tom

We didn't always enjoy each other this much.

Eric

And we get to spend time with our mom and dad. It's just a wonderful situation.

Roots

Would you recommend that young people work in the food industry?

Eric

Absolutely. I strongly recommend taking advantage of the service culture here in Chelan. It's a skill set that makes everything else better. You'll be better off at everything. Better at conversations. More confident. And you have a sense of value about how to treat people. We're a Golden Rule business. Treat people the way you want to be treated.

Tom

That's what Dad always told us, and his dad told him, and all the way back. Family motto. Treat people the way you want to be treated.

CJ'S GRILL

CJ's Grill

LeeAnne Weathersby was our first official interview for this project, and what a great way to start it off. Her story is a compelling one, filled with successes and real tragedies. She was generous enough to bring the entire class a tray filled with homemade cinnamon rolls. There are few things a group of middle schoolers like more than cinnamon rolls. Our conversation spanned a wide range of topics, from her family's experiences during Hurricane Katrina to her long-standing interest in food and small town business.

Roots

How would you describe the food you serve?

LeeAnne

It's a wide range. We have everything from pancakes to biscuits and gravy, hamburgers and salads, Cajun Creole and Southern style food. Gumbo, that sort of thing. There isn't anyone in the Valley who does Southern food, and we've tried to carve out a little niche.

Many people around here don't know much about Southern food. Or they think they know about it from TV. So we're trying to educate people in a way, give them some exposure to homestyle Southern cooking.

And we're obviously trying to do something different from what's already been done here in Chelan. Chelan has lots of pizza, lots of Mexican, a few Italian spots now. We're trying to do something different and put our own rung on the ladder.

Roots

Are you from the South?

LeeAnne

I was born and raised here in Chelan. But I moved to Mississippi in my 20s and lived there for 18 years. I was there until Hurricane Katrina hit and blew my house away to somewhere else. After that we came back here.

Roots

That was in 2005?

LeeAnne

Right. September 2005 we moved back. For 15 years we watched the storms come through. We'd watch on the TV, right? The storm's coming this way, the storm's coming that way. If you don't know how a hurricane works, it rotates in a clockwise direction, and the inner circle, the eye, there's nothing happening in the eye. But all around it are what they call bands, and those bands lift the water up and they bring rain and water and flooding.

Katrina was huge. It took over three states. The eye went right through Waverly where we lived. And those tight inner bands hit us hard.

We were two blocks from the beach. We ended up leaving. We discussed it a lot as a family whether we were going to leave or not. For years the storms had come and we had stayed. At first we thought, nah, we'll ride this one out. But eventually we changed our minds and we went to Georgia to wait.

On the way back, about five days after we left, we found bridges all washed out. We knew it was bad. And our house was just gone. Just gone. Whole house just blown away to Iowa or somewhere. The only thing left was the swimming pool out back.

So you go: what do we do? And our kids, they're young at the time, and they're seeing friends of theirs who had stayed and who didn't make it. Neighbors who had stayed and didn't make it. Nobody who stayed on our block survived. It was incredibly hard. My oldest, it really messed with his head. Messed with all our heads, really.

Roots
Why did you open CJ's?

LeeAnne
Darn good question. Sometimes I wonder that myself. You know, opening a business is a coin toss. It's 50/50 whether it's a good thing to do or not. Mostly we wanted to introduce what we knew about food and cooking to the community.

Roots
Can you talk about the style of cooking you learned down South?

LeeAnne
It was my husband's family mostly that taught me down South, and a little old lady next door that I learned from as well. I wanted to learn, right? I watched other people cooking and pitched in and learned by watching and doing.

Down South they love food like you can't explain. They love to get together. It's a whole different culture than anywhere else.

Roots
What did you do before getting into the restaurant industry?

LeeAnne
I owned a gym here in town for nine years. Right across from the Shell station where the screen printing place is now.

Roots

Which do you prefer?

LeeAnne

It's hard. At the gym, I learned a lot about health and working out and all that stuff. I gained a lot of knowledge from doing that. And I got to help people on the fitness side of things, and I absolutely loved engaging with people in that way. But my joy is cooking. And I was always cooking anyway when I wasn't at the gym.

Roots

What's a normal day look like for you?

LeeAnne

I'm usually starting at 6:00. I work for Okanogan County Transportation and Nutrition. I cover Chelan and Douglas Counties, from Chelan up to Waterville and around Crescent Bar and all the way over to Leavenworth. There are about 400 seniors on my program. We cook and deliver meals to those elderly people who can't get out of their houses. So I'll be doing that until around 5:00.

Then I'm at the restaurant, where I cook until around 8:30 or 9:00. Then there's always a little paperwork to be done. That usually takes until 10:00 or so. That's Monday through Friday. Saturdays and Sundays I'm at the restaurant all day.

Roots

What surprised you the most in opening a restaurant?

LeeAnne

I think finding that people actually enjoy your food and are willing to come and purchase it. Even though in your head you know you've made something right, you've cooked something that tastes good. But you never know how your taste is going to compare to someone else's. You just never know if it's going to please the customers. So the fact that it does, that's just a surprise and a relief.

Roots

How did you craft your menu?

LeeAnne

I took all the food I've loved to eat over the years and tried to adapt it to something that would be unique and enjoyable. For example, we have a Monte Cristo sandwich on our menu. Most people around here don't have that on their menu.

The first time I ate a Monte Cristo I was 13 and it was at a restaurant right here in Chelan called The Crockery. They're no longer in business. And I thought about that sandwich and how much I loved it and I said: I'm going to recreate that and make my own version. And it's one of our biggest sellers.

Roots

How did you come up with the name CJ's?

LeeAnee

CJ's is for my youngest son: Christopher Jarod. He had opened up a concession stand at Don Morse Park when he was 14. He got a business license, paid taxes, everything. All the money he made for those four years went towards his college.

And then I took it over when he graduated. At the time we were starting our restaurant on the golf course, and we thought: why change the name? We can use the same name and keep the business license current. So we had CJ's By the Lake and CJ's on the Course. When we decided to close up shop on the golf course and start a business downtown, we did the same thing. Now we're CJ's Grill.

Roots

Were you interested in cooking as a kid?

LeeAnne

I learned a lot about cooking from my grandmother. I spent my summers in Alaska. I was in the Kodiak Islands in Coughlin Cove, which is a logging camp. No grocery stores, no telephones, nothing. My grandmother taught me to cook biscuits and gravy, the kind of stuff she'd cook for my grandfather before he went out logging.

Roots

Can you speak to the differences between Chelan and where you lived in Mississippi?

LeeAnne

I really think down South there's a sense of community that is just really unique. You could be outside doing a barbecue or a crawfish boil and before you know it the whole neighborhood is standing in your backyard.

But Chelan is something really special too. And I remember when I was down South that I always missed the seasons. The seasons and the sidewalks. I know that sounds silly, but sidewalks don't exist down South. I missed snow and sidewalks.

We actually went back about five years ago. The hurricane had just wiped out the entire town. And so they had to rebuild the whole thing, and it's just nothing like what it was before. They built freeways and interchanges and tall buildings and it's just not the same town.

That's one thing I love about Chelan. It's changed a lot, but there's no freeways. So I'm happy.

COMPANY CREEK

Company Creek Pizza

I met with Keith Jenkins, the owner of Company Creek Pizza, and Brooke Dodson, the manager, early in the spring. I'd been admiring all of the history on the walls – photos of old Chelan Goats basketball teams, football teams and newspaper cutouts from decades before – while Keith and Brooke got settled.

Company Creek has been a staple in Chelan for over 50 years, so the pictures on the walls aren't just for show. It stands as the longest running pizza restaurant in town, and one of the longest running businesses period. We sat at a table by the wall under the faded picture of a Chelan high schooler who eventually went on to pitch in the major leagues.

Beau:
When did you open Company Creek pizza?

Keith:
Actually I didn't open Company Creek. I bought it in 2006. Originally it opened in 1971.

Beau:
What's your role in the restaurant?

Keith:
I'm the owner. Brooke here is the manager. Being the owner sounds nice, but really it just means that you have to do a little of everything.

Beau:
Why did you decide to buy Company Creek?

Keith:
Good question. No idea. That was 2006. Do you remember anything about why you did something in 2006.

Beau:
No. I wasn't alive.

Keith:
Well there you go. I don't remember. Probably it seemed like a good idea at the time.

Beau:
How many employees do you have?

Keith:
I'd say 20. It fluctuates, but I think it's right around 20.

Brooke:
Yeah, it's 20.

Beau:
How would you describe the food you serve?

Keith:
Pizza, hamburgers, pasta. It's pretty straightforward. We don't necessarily do anything fancy, but we try to provide options for people and give them good quality at a reasonable price.

Brooke:
There are a lot of pizza restaurants in Chelan, but I think what sets us apart is how many other things we have on our menu. The other pizza places don't do burgers. They don't do french fries.

Beau:
What's your favorite thing on the menu?

Keith:
The Alfredo garlic pasta. It's fantastic.

Brooke:
The cinnamon bites.

Beau:
You have cinnamon bites?

Brooke:
Yep. Told you we have a lot of options.

Beau:
I like cinnamon bites.

Keith:
Who doesn't? You should try the mushroom Swiss burger. It's another one that's really good. Easy to overlook. You go to a pizza joint, you don't necessarily think mushroom Swiss burger.

Beau:
Is there anything on the menu that's harder to cook?

Keith:
The pastas can be difficult. They're made from scratch. That always complicates things.

Beau:
How did you create your menu?

Keith:
Honestly, we didn't need to recreate the menu. We took what the menu had been when I bought the place and have kept it pretty steady ever since.

Brooke:
I'd say people have a certain expectation of the kind of food they'll get here. Company Creek's been around a long time. And we've tried to improve on the quality of the food. I think the food you're getting here now is much better than what you'd have gotten twenty years ago.

But you can only change it so much.

Keith:
Right. Change it too much and people aren't happy.

Beau:
Do you like running a restaurant in Chelan?

Keith:
I do. It's very rewarding. What we do here, we really try to connect with the locals. Obviously we serve a lot of tourists in the summer, but we really make an effort to build relationships with the locals. We have a lot of groups that come in regularly, a lot of old timers, and this is a special place for them.

We try to be a place for families, for kids. We get a lot of birthdays, that sort of thing. It's very rewarding.

Beau:
What's a normal day look like for you?

Keith:
Quieter in the morning. We sell a lot of burgers at lunch, pizza in the evenings. In the summer it's busy busy. Like I said, I do a bit of everything, so there's always plenty to do.

Beau:
What was the biggest surprise about running a restaurant?

Keith:
How busy it is in the summer. Honestly, Chelan has always been busy in the summers, of course, but the level of activity has just really increased. There's no letdown anymore. And the shoulder seasons have become busier too.

Beau:
What did you do before purchasing Company Creek?

Keith:
Bookkeeping. I wanted to be an accountant.

Beau:
Did you always want to own a restaurant?

Keith:
No. I definitely wanted to be an accountant.

Beau:
Gotcha. Is accounting an easy profession?

Keith:
Nope. It's incredibly time consuming.

Beau:
Why should people come to Company Creek?

Keith:
Well, it's a fun place. The food is quality and the price is affordable. We're very kid friendly. We're a good place for families. You can see there's lots of room, space to spread out.

Brooke:
Agreed. People should come if they want a relaxed dining experience and lots of options for food. We have good service, low prices, and we always try to treat people right.

312 E WOODIN AVE
COUNTYLINECHELAN.COM
509-682-2828

COUNTY LINE

County Line

Josh and Allison Flaten joined us at Roots Community School for the following interview. In addition, they also hosted us at their fabulous restaurant, County Line, and gave us a full tour of their facilities, including their Nomad Food Truck. We tried their Smoked Mac & Cheese and their Jalapeno Poppers, both of which were hits. Like a number of owners we spoke to, the Flatens opened their doors during the pandemic, a particularly trying time to run a restaurant.

Roots

You said you left a job after 22 years and then came to Chelan. Can you speak to where you're from and what you were doing before the move?

Allison

Sure. We are both originally from the Issaquah area. We'd lived in Covington. Josh was working at Snoqualmie Pass, and I was in HR. Still am. I'm the head of HR for a consulting firm where I work remote, so it wasn't an issue for me to move really, but it was a significant change for Josh.

But we were looking for a change. On the West side it's dark and gloomy the majority of the year. We were just tired of the traffic, the rain, all of it. Josh's parents had moved here about nine years ago, and they'd said we should try it out. And then one day, Josh was scrolling through properties online and found the building up for sale, and it just seemed like a great opportunity.

Josh

I did 22 years at Snoqualmie in food and beverage. Last 12 years I was lodge manager and food and beverage manager. We had four different base areas under one umbrella, so I spent a lot of time in kitchens and cafeterias.

I got to the point where I realized I was doing all this work for somebody else and could be doing it for myself on a lot smaller operation. At Snoqualmie it was three kitchens, two bars, an espresso, a cafe, a cart, 45 to 50 employees, over 8,000 square feet of dining space. Now I've got 2,000 feet of dining space and no more than fifteen employees. One kitchen. One bar. It's smaller, but it's ours.

Roots

What kind of food do you guys specialize in?

Josh

We have things from all over the place. We have a Poke Bowl. Or take our Woodin Noodle Salad. Real Asian themes. But we also have Mediterranean Greek food, and some comfort food like our Smoked Mac & Cheese. We've got a French Dip.

Allison

We have a lot of rotating stuff. We just put beets on the menu with a pear vinaigrette. We like to keep things fresh with the seasons and change things up.

Roots

Why did you decide to start a restaurant?

Allison

When I was growing up, I actually thought I wanted to go into culinary arts. My senior year I did a Home Economics class which was really just cooking. I always loved to cook. Josh, he enjoys smoking and doing the proteins, but we love cooking together. And we also had been working in customer service pretty much our entire lives. I was 14 when I started, and Josh just about the same.

Josh

There's the social aspect too. Being part of the community. A restaurant is a kind of hub for the community, a gathering space to come hang out and do fun things together. But it's definitely not for the lighthearted. It's a hustle. And it's a labor of love. There's a daily grind, although most days I'd say it doesn't feel like work.

Roots

Were there lessons you took from your years at Snoqualmie?

Josh

Up there on the mountain, you're on your own in a lot of ways. The facilities are old, the equipment's old. So you have to be a jack of all trades, a master of none. You have to know some plumbing and some basic kitchen repair, that sort of thing.

You also learn a lot of quick service stuff. We had satellite kitchens up there, small restaurants basically that would pump out lots of food in short amounts of time. We had an oven that just sat at 500 degrees. It could jump to 700 degrees and do radiant and convection, just stirring air around so the hot air distributed evenly. And we got one of those for County Line. It gets our sandwiches out a lot faster.

Roots

You guys have a pretty unique kitchen.

Josh

It is. There's no hood system, so we can't have fryers or cook raw proteins inside. That's why we use the smoker for a lot of our raw proteins. You have to be very creative with the menu when you don't have a fryer.

Allison

Lots of people want french fries, which we can't do. So we do potato chips with a house dip instead. We had to really think outside the box to provide creative food with the equipment we have.

Josh

Right now we use a pellet smoker for our proteins. And we have a convection oven. We're able to cook a lot of things that don't require a hood.

Roots

Are customers disappointed when they don't see fries on the menu?

Josh

Sometimes. Sometimes they leave. It happens.

Roots

How did you decide to serve the particular cuisine you serve?

Allison

If you're going out to eat in Chelan, you see a lot of similarities in the food. There's a lot of pizza, a lot of Mexican cuisine. Burgers. Which is all great. But we wanted to do food that we love. We're passionate about food. And we wanted to do something different. One thing we noticed was the lack of variety, and so we wanted to bring that to the community. Hence our Poke Bowl, our Greek Gyro, our Farro Salad.

Roots

What do you like most about owning a restaurant?

Josh

I'd say the people, for sure. The opportunity to see so many people throughout the community. Chelan is a destination location in the summer. Pretty much every week you've got people coming to visit, so there's a real fun social part of it. And being creative with food and the drinks.

Roots

Had you been to Chelan before moving here to start County Line?

Josh

My family started coming in the 70s. My grandparents bought a timeshare at Wapato Point. I think the first time I came was in August of 1983. Somewhere along the way I realized this is exactly what we wanted to be a part of: a small community where we could do fun things like this interview with you guys, and be a part of something, and cook great food, all of it.

Allison

I had never actually been to Chelan until I went with Josh's parents. We came to visit just a couple years ago. But before that, no. My sister had friends who came here in the summers. I was always jealous of them getting to come and hang out at the lake.

Roots

What's a normal day look like for you?

Josh

Every day is similar. I show up and talk to my crew, find out where they're at. I'll look at sales from the previous day and go through any orders that need to be done. Then I'm in the kitchen for a few hours prepping: slice and dice, season, portion, blend, all of that until around noon. Then there's emails to answer. I may do some service stuff if the staff needs it. Then take a break for a few hours and then back on in late afternoon or early evening to help with the rush. That's five days a week.

Roots

What was the biggest surprise opening your own restaurant?

Josh

I think the biggest thing is it's your own money. Before, at Snoqualmie, you know you're ordering or making purchase requests, but it's not your money.

Allison

For me it was setting up payroll. I've worked HR, but I never ran payroll. There's so much that's not necessarily hard but you have to learn all these new things: licensing permits, dealing with the health department, dealing with the city.

Josh

Fun stuff like going through an extensive background check and finding out how many speeding tickets you actually have.

Roots

If you have too many speeding tickets do you not get your liquor license?

Josh

Not for speeding. But like DUI or assault charges, theft, that sort of thing.

Roots

Can you tell us about your food truck?

Josh

With the food truck, everyone thinks you just roll up and start serving food. They don't think about how much prep there is, and also ensuring that the truck has fuel, that it has water. You have to have a drain for your gray water. On and on.

Allison

Or how hot it is in there. People never realize that.

Josh

You talk about heat. We have an AC unit, but it doesn't put out nearly enough. There's a fryer in the truck running at 350 degrees. And the flat top at 400 degrees. Plus it's 100 degrees outside in the summer. That food truck is a sweat box. We had it up to 117 degrees inside there before.

Allison

Every time you're setting up the mobile, it's a new location. You've got to factor in so many things, and if you forget something you're in real trouble.

Josh

One time we were driving to Wenatchee and our fridge didn't latch. We open up and we've got diced tomatoes everywhere, and I'm running to the US Foods ChefStore to buy cherry tomatoes because they're easier to dice. Everything's just more complicated. It's an 18-foot long kitchen, but you've got three people inside. It's tight.

Roots

What do you like most about running a business in Chelan?

Josh

It's beautiful being here. Being part of this community is fantastic. Giving back to the community is the best part. Like we do meals for Thrive. We recently donated a new scoreboard for the baseball team. Doing things like this, sitting here with you guys.

Allison

Connecting to the community, for sure. We have regulars who are in every Monday for lunch like clockwork, or they come in every day and hang out at the bar for an hour or two after work. That kind of thing. So you get to know people.

Roots

What was it like transforming a house into a restaurant?

Allison

A lot of it had been done by the previous operation, Shot of Gratitude. They'd removed the walls and put beams in to support the roof. Removing the tub, making the bathroom smaller, placing the floor sinks, that sort of thing.

Josh

In a restaurant, they have a thing called an air gap. Your kitchen sinks, your ice maker, your dishwasher, they can't all be direct plumbing that goes into the house. There has to be an air gap. That way if there's a clog and something backs up, you're not putting sewage or wastewater into your sinks.

And you have to have a grease trap. It's the last line of defense before water goes into the main sewer. You have to clean that baby once or twice a year.

Allison

It's foul. But every restaurant has to have one. And once you clean it, you wish you never had to do it again.

Josh

We also redid everything aesthetically. I put built-in benches in the front dining room and in the back. We built tables for the inside and out front. We had to create a bar space, put in a walk-in refrigerator out back, a draft system for beverages. Stereo equipment, speakers, TVs, all of it.

Roots

How did you guys manage to get through the pandemic? You were opening right when the pandemic was taking off.

Allison

It was a real holy crap moment. We'd just sold our house, and we took out a loan from our 401K, and all the equity we poured into the remodel. So we were freaking out.

Josh

We were operating outside in the winter. That was really challenging. We closed for three weeks, and about 10 days in we talked to people around town, friends of ours, and they kept saying: Josh, there's nowhere to go. We need a place to go.

So we put on our big boy pants and spent the money to create an outdoor environment. Somewhere close to $10,000. Two tents, gas fireplaces, propane heaters. We had 16 propane tanks, like $60 to $160 a day on propane. Two TVs outside so people could watch football. It was a struggle, but we did good. We kept four employees going at 30 hours per week. And we operated in the black.

Allison

If you're operating in the green, you're making money. In the red, you're losing money. In the black, you're treading water. But you're keeping the doors open and keeping your employees employed.

Roots

You've stuck with a digital menu even after the pandemic rather than returning to paper ones. What was the reason for that?

Josh

Well during the pandemic it was single-use menus. That was the requirement. Use it and throw it away. So we were going through about $160 a month in menus. But after that was lifted, it still made sense for us to go with the online menu because our menu actually changes quite often.

Our drink list changes. Our rotating taps change in the summer constantly. The wine changes. And our food too. We might run out of something and then it's not on the menu the rest of the day. With the online menu, we can update it in real time so our servers don't have to say: hey, sorry, we're out of this item.

But we're making a number of updates right now, some big menu changes. So come on by here in the next few months and check it out. There'll be some fun new stuff on the menu here in the spring.

DEB'S DELIGHTS

Deb's Delights

I met Debbi Clark, the owner of Deb's Delights, on a rare sunny Wednesday in March. She mentioned that she isn't fond of sharing her recipes, but in our case she was willing to make an exception. "For a community cookbook, I'm willing to break the rules," she said. Debbi said she didn't originally intend to become a baker. She had meant to be a midwife. But fate had other plans. Which is lucky for us, because her chocolate mousse is absolutely delicious.

Grace:
How does a normal day look for you?

Deb's Delights:
I try get the baking done before noon because it gets so hot. Then I'm either baking or decorating cakes or checking emails or answering the phones. People are coming in and out, ordering or most of the time picking up desserts. Then I go home and try to get some sleep.

Grace:
What were you most surprised by once you opened the restaurant?

Deb's Delights:
How hard it is to be a business owner in general.

Grace:
How did you create your menu?

Deb's Delights:
I based it on things that I like. It's really just all my favorite things.

Grace:
Are cakes and pastries your favorite foods?

Deb's Delights:
Actually they're not. They're what I'm good at, but I don't have much of a sweet tooth. Which is kinda odd for a baker, right? I spend all day making cakes and goodies, but I don't eat much of them myself.

Grace:
What is your favorite thing to bake?

Deb's Delights:
Well, my favorite dessert is Swedish Cream.

Grace:
Sounds yummy. What's your favorite thing to eat that's not a dessert?

Deb's Delights:
Just in general? Sushi.

Grace:
We don't have that here in Chelan. We really could use a sushi restaurant. What's the hardest thing for you to bake?

Deb's Delights:
The hardest? I would say cakes that are covered in fondant.

Grace:
I watch a lot of baking shows, and it certainly looks like people struggle with fondant a lot.

Deb's Delights:
Yeah, fondant has a mind of its own.

Grace:
What makes it so tricky?

Deb's Delights:
It gets hard. You have to work it and work fast and hope that it likes you that day. If it doesn't, then it isn't going to work out.

Grace:
What do you like about running a restaurant in Chelan?

Deb's Delights:
I love the community. The people here are just fantastic and very supportive.

Grace:
Did you always want to own a restaurant?

Deb's Delights:
No. Actually not. I was going to be a midwife, believe it or not.

Grace:
Why should people come to Deb's Delights?

Deb's Delights:
Well, I'd say the food is really good. If you want really high-quality cakes or pastries. Who doesn't like a good pastry?

Grace:
How did you start as a baker?

Deb's Delights:
Wedding cakes. I've been making wedding cakes for 26 years. I was working out of my home making cakes, three or four every summer. A friend of mine was a florist and she was doing a wedding with a bride who had very little money. She wanted to know if I'd make a cake for her. My friend knew I was pretty good with cakes. And that's really where it started, with wedding cakes. Later I became a pastry chef. And that led to opening my own place.

Grace:
This is an interesting building for a bakery. What was it originally? A garage?

Deb's Delights:
Yeah, attached to the house. It was their garage and they had it converted into a commercial kitchen for somebody else who baked bread and then it was empty for a long time. And then I came in.

Grace:
Have you ever wanted more partners or more people to work with you?

Deb's Delights:
I've thought about it, but I'm way too controlling. I find I can't let stuff go. It's my name on the door, right? So I'm not sure it would work out well. I'd rather just work really hard and get it done rather than have to micromanage someone else.

Grace:
I was looking at some of your cakes back there. There was a bunch with the flowers on them. What's with all the flowers? Is that like a special request?

Deb's Delights:
So those cakes there are just display cakes. I did a wedding show. I was a vendor at a wedding show a few weeks ago. And so I took those to decorate my booth with. And so when my customers come in, brides and grooms who come in to taste, they can see what I can do and get ideas.

Grace:
I see. They're very pretty.

Deb's Delights:
So those are just like silk flowers. Normally people use fresh flowers for on their wedding cakes. It really is funny because I never thought 26 years ago that making a cake for friend would go this far, and now here I am running booths for wedding cakes. Who would have guessed?

GOLDIE'S

Goldie's

I met Jill Pollard at Goldies on 106 East Woodin Avenue. Opening Goldies was the main reason Jill and her family moved from Kauai in Hawaii all the way across the ocean to Chelan. Visiting Chelan previously she had realized the Valley was without an acai bowl cafe, and she decided to fix that problem. Moving here, Jill purchased the Goldsmith Lucerne building and split it into two separate businesses: Goldies and Moonpenny.

Opening Moonpenny was actually less complicated, but Jill finds Goldies more fulfilling. Watching the look of satisfaction on people's faces as they eat is fulfilling and rewarding.

Logan
You guys opened in 2020?

Goldies
Correct. COVID hit earlier that year, and I opened in November. Opening a new business in November is a great little warm-up trial to get your legs under you. Our experience was pretty positive.

Logan
Which business did you open first?

Goldies
Moonpenny. It opened in July of 2020. And then on the Goldies side we couldn't have opened because we were still remodeling. We were adding walls, putting in the archway, adding bathrooms.

Logan
Which have you enjoyed more?

Goldies
They're so different. I can make a lot more money at Moonpenny because I have a lot of stuff people can buy, more options. And people can order stuff through Moonpenny that we might not have in the store right then. With Goldies, people have to order straight from the menu and it's made on the spot.

I like to think of myself as a very creative person. I like each business for different reasons. I love food. I love clothes. It's great to be able to do both.

Logan
How many employees do you have?

Goldies

It's a big swing between summer and winter. In the off season, when we're open, I usually have one employee. Just Goldies we're talking about. And in the summer I might have 10.

Logan

How would you describe the food you serve?

Goldies

Acai bowls and smoothies. We do have coffee and a few other drinks, but it's mainly acai bowls and smoothies.

Logan

Why did you start an acai bowl cafe?

Goldies

We were living in Kauai in Hawaii. One of our favorite things there was eating acai bowls. I had worked for an acai bowl cafe and managed it there and just fell in love with the whole concept.

We visited Chelan one year, and as we were walking around I just thought: this place should have an acai bowl cafe. And I just kind of said, well, we should move here and open one.

Logan

What did you do before you went into the restaurant business?

Goldies

I hosted women's retreats where women could come and do wellness stuff. I was a health coach. I've always been very into health and wellness.

That background has obviously been useful with Goldies. I'm very passionate about food, but also I'm very picky. A lot of the food industry serves you stuff that's not particularly healthy. Lots of grease and oils. We don't use any hydrogenated oils at Goldies, only coconut and avocado oils.

When I opened Goldies, the main reason was because I thought people deserved a place to eat where the food was high quality and very health conscious.

Logan

Where are you from originally?

Goldies

I grew up in Redmond, here in Washington. I actually get to see a lot of my friends from Redmond every summer. They vacation here and come in and we get to say hi.

BEAR FOODS

MARKET · Mercantile · Crêperie

CRÊPERIE

OPEN - Th_____ay 10-2 PM

CRÊPERIE TEMPORARILY
CLOSED
We apologize for any inconvenience.

Step inside & get lost for a while...

Logan
What do you like most about owning a restaurant?

Goldies
Making people happy with food. That is very rewarding.

Logan
What's a normal day look like for you?

Goldies
It takes about half an hour to get set up before we open. Then we're open by 9:00. Things start to get really busy around 10:00 and on through 1:00.

Our menu is pretty limited, so everyone wears all the hats. For each employee, you could be taking orders. You could be blending. You could be doing the dishes. You could be topping the bowls. Everyone participates in each stage. It's not divided up. And by the end of the day you're cleaning bathrooms. When we close up, it takes about an hour to clean up. We've got to restock, mop, all that stuff.

You asked what my favorite part of the job was. Well, I'd say my second favorite part is working with my staff. These guys have stayed with me a long time, and I just adore them and all the work they do here.

Logan
What surprised you the most about owning a restaurant?

Goldies
I think because we had the comparison of the two businesses, what surprised me was how much harder it is to run a restaurant. Selling clothes isn't exactly ridiculously hard. With the restaurant, the real challenge is getting people to know we're here. People are still discovering us all the time. Which is great, but it's a challenge to make sure your name is out there and people know you exist.

Probably I need to get onto KOZI even more in the summers, just to make sure people continue to hear about us.

Logan
Do you have a favorite item on the menu?

Goldies
I love the Golden Bowl. It's an acai bowl with peanut butter, strawberries and banana.

Logan
What's the most difficult thing on your menu to make?

Goldies

Well, it's physically hard to blend the smoothies. That's probably the biggest challenge for the employees. The other thing is our baker. Not that any one thing for her is hard, but there are some challenges. Like she has to make homemade almond butter, which takes like 25 minutes. You have to emulsify the almonds and grind them down until they become oily. That's a challenge.

Logan

Do you enjoy how busy the summers are in Chelan?

Goldies

I do. It sounds crazy, but I enjoy the energy of it, the excitement. And now we've been in business a few years, so we have returning customers, and that's fun to build relationships with those people who come year after year.

Logan

Did you always want to own a restaurant?

Goldies

I didn't actually think about it until 2019. That was the first time I considered the idea. When I was little, I never said: oh, I'm going to own a restaurant some day! So this kind of came out of left field.

Logan

Why should people come to Goldies?

Goldies

In the summer, I'd say to people they should come to cool down. Getting a smoothie or an acai bowl is literally cooling. Refreshing is probably a better word. And it's healthy. I'd say if you were interested in food that's healthy and refreshing, you should give us a shot.

510 E WOODIN AVE
LAGOPASTA.COM
509-910-0141

LAGO PASTA

Lago Pasta

We sat down with Nathan Gottlieb, who along with Teague Block owns Lago Pasta. In addition to our interview, Nathan and Teague took the time to have us back again for a tour of their facilities, going as far as taking apart their pasta machine to show us exactly how it makes all of their wonderful pasta.

Later in the year, when one of our team returned to buy pasta, Teague invited him to throw on some gloves and come behind the counter and gave him a one-on-one lesson on precisely how to make their fantastic Pomodoro sauce.

Roots

You guys opened in 2023. How did you and Teague meet and decide to start a pasta restaurant?

Nathan

Teague and I have known each other since we were about six years old. We grew up in Port Townsend on Bainbridge on the peninsula. Teague and I were in little league together. His dad was our coach. Teague's family owned a feed store. They only sold it just a few years ago. Bay Hay and Feed Store. They owned it for like 40 years.

I owned a business in Pike Place Market: Pasta Casalinga. It's still there. And Teague was doing paddle boarding and kayak rentals here in Chelan. A place called Lake Rider. After he sold Lake Rider, Teague kept saying I ought to come out here to Chelan. That we ought to start a restaurant. Which was the right time for me, really. I was tired of Seattle. I love that city. Love it. But I was tired of a lot of what was going on there and looking for a change. So I sold my part of Pasta Casalinga, and the rest is history.

Roots

So you've been cooking pasta for some time then.

Nathan

I've been in the industry since I was 16. My background is actually in Neapolitan pizza. I love wood-fired pizza. But I spent the last seven years getting deep into pasta.

Roots

Do you have a favorite item on the menu?

Nathan

The Pomodoro for sure. I love playing with food and coming up with new things. But the Pomodoro is just such a fantastic sauce. I use these tomatoes out of Italy. There's these two brothers in Naples, and they're just the best canned tomatoes you can buy. Simple and delicious. That's the key, really. The simpler the food, the better it is.

Roots

What was the most surprising thing about opening a restaurant here in Chelan?

Nathan

I couldn't believe how much the local community supported us from day one. I don't know if you noticed, but outside, we don't even have a sign. People just found us from day one, and the word spread, and the support has just been amazing. You expect when you open it's going to take some time to build a reputation. So the biggest surprise was just how quickly the community embraced what we were doing and came to support us.

When we opened, we thought we'd be doing 30 to 40 pastas a day. That would have been a good start. But we were doing 100 to 150 every day.

Roots

How do you craft your menu?

Nathan

Our menu is an interesting thing. The whole concept is we're always going to have the Pomodoro, but then we want to take advantage of what's seasonal. We're always experimenting. We have new things for people to try, and then we see what they like and what they don't. And we have a number of add-ons so people can change it up to their personal taste, right? Extra cheese, extra sauce, chili oil, all that kind of stuff.

We just started doing lasagnas, so we're seeing how that goes. It's been hard to keep up with so far. People love it. So that may become a standard. We'll have to see.

Roots

What is your specific role in the business?

Nathan

Number one would be the chef. But my speciality lies in numbers and accounting. Teague and I, we do everything together. So it's not really one person plays just one role. We're a team. But I'm more a food person, and Teague is more a visionary person. He's got the mind for construction, layouts, all that kind of thing.

Roots

Can you compare owning a restaurant in Seattle and here?

Nathan

Well my restaurant in Pike Place, that was incredible. Seattle is a great place, and there's always so many different kinds of people you're meeting and talking to. There's an energy there. But I love the community out here. I love how connected it is, how tight-knit everybody is. It's got a wonderful vibe that's much different from the city.

Roots
What drew you to wanting to work in the restaurant industry?

Nathan
I played a lot of team sports as a kid. And restaurants are basically like that. It's very similar. There's leadership, camaraderie, lots of different people with different backgrounds and skill sets. Every day you come to work and you play with your team.

Roots
Tell us about this building. This doesn't look like your typical restaurant.

Nathan
It used to be a karate studio. In the back parking lot, you can actually still see the studio logo on the concrete.

This is actually Teague's house. He owns the building and lives upstairs. We joke that when someone sits down and eats here, they're literally sitting down at Teague's table and having dinner in his house.

But we both put money into it, of course, to buy equipment, renovate and all that. The pasta machine alone cost $40,000. More than the money, though, we both brought a lot of experience. In my case, I've been 20 years in the restaurant industry, so that was the greatest capital I could bring to the table. Experience and knowledge.

Roots
Why should people go to Pasta Lago?

Nathan
It's a fun place. It's reasonably priced. That's a big thing for us. When we were first looking around Chelan, we noticed a lot of restaurants are really pricey. What we wanted to make was something that was accessible to people from all different backgrounds. That was important to us from the start.

Roots
Can you speak to where you source your ingredients and products from?

Nathan
Sourcing is interesting. In the summer, we work a lot with local farmers. We get a lot of stuff that's grown right here in the area. Fresh stuff. For specialty products, I was in food import and distribution for six years, and so I have a lot of connections there in the industry. A lot of small producers and importers that I'm able to connect with. I think we work with between 15 and 20 different companies that we buy product from.

Like with Seattle importers right now, we're looking at small producers of canned fish, that sort of thing. You're always looking, always networking, always researching.

Sometimes it's just better products, or maybe it's better prices. And I'm very picky. Like with our tomatoes. They have to be San Marzano. Anything else is lower quality, and I can't have it. That's the biggest thing with cooking. Quality products.

Roots

What do you enjoy most about owning a restaurant?

Nathan

I love being my own boss. I love the excitement. It's exhilarating because it's a big risk. Any kind of business, but especially restaurants, there's a huge risk. It may not work out, right? You come in and you feel you have to perform and be on your best every day. Otherwise how are you going to pay the rent? So I love that excitement.

Roots

Are there any unique challenges to owning a restaurant in Chelan?

Nathan

One thing I've noticed is that there isn't a natural flow to the customers coming in. Sometimes it's slow, sometime's it's super busy. Or it gets incredibly busy all of a sudden, which makes it hard to plan for and produce food in an orderly fashion.

Roots

How much pasta do you make in a week?

Nathan

Like in the summer? Probably around 200 pounds a day. We make pasta for ourselves, obviously, and then we supply some of the local restaurants like Campbell's and Siren Song. Our goal from the start was to actually do two things: the restaurant, and then the wholesale pasta supply. But the restaurant got so busy the wholesale had to be put on the back burner.

Roots

What is your pasta made from?

Nathan

It's a semolina pasta. Semolina and water.

Roots

Would you say that your approach to pasta is traditional?

Nathan

It depends. When it comes to pasta, we follow a lot of the rules, so to speak. But not always to the T. Some of my Italian friends, they don't care for what we do. They have their own opinions. But you have to do it your own way. Sometimes that means bucking tradition. You gotta go your own way.

LOCAL MYTH

Local Myth Pizza

For this interview we ventured to Local Myth Pizza to meet with Bob and Caden Doggett and Madison MacKenzie, owners and managers of both Local Myth Pizza, located downtown Chelan, and Cafe Myth, located on the lower level of Benson Winery. Our hosts were gracious enough to host a short pizza making seminar there in the kitchen and allow us to taste some of their fabulous pizza.

Roots

When did you purchase Local Myth?

Bob

So the restaurant originally opened in 1997, and then we purchased the restaurant from Art in 2013. And we opened Cafe Myth up at Benson in 2019. We were going to open that earlier but COVID delayed our opening.

Roots

What makes your pizza distinct?

Bob

Great question. We do two unique styles of pizza. What we do here is called West Coast Artisan. New York style would be a bit of a thinner crust and baked around 600 degrees. Chicago, now that's a deep dish pizza. With Chicago, you layer your ingredients and the sauce goes on top. Ours, what we do, is we make everything from scratch. We make dough every day. We make sauce every day. Our pizza is rolled and hand tossed. It's a thinner style of pizza, cooked about 625 degrees. We do sauce on bottom and toppings on top of that. The dough is very important. Dough, and the quality of your sauce and cheese. That's the three most important things.

Caden

If you think about a pizza, it's like building a house. The foundation is the dough and the sauce and the cheese. Then you're putting toppings on. If you can make the best cheese pizza in the world, you're going to have a great pizza, right? Because you've got that foundation. It's got to be good.

Bob

This dough here, we age it for 24 hours. That aging is called fermentation. It's fermenting and it gets a little more sour as you go. That brings flavor into the dough. The flavor is all about the ingredients and the fermentation: honey, olive oil, flour, sugar, salt, water, yeast.

Up at Benson, we use only flour, water, salt and yeast, but the flour is super fine ground. It's actually a flour from Naples, and the water is well-water from the vineyard.

Caden

That dough ages for 72 hours, though. A good four days.

Bob

Exactly. It's building flavor. The pizza we're doing at Benson, it's a different style from what we're doing here at Local Myth. Up there it's Neapolitan style.

Madison

I think the other thing that makes us unique is that everything is made from scratch. We use some really unique pizza sauces, and those are all our own. Our recipes are very different from what you'll find in almost any other restaurant.

Roots

How did you get into the cooking industry?

Bob

I've always been passionate about food. I was a competitive cook here in Washington and down in Texas. I competed in chili cook-offs, barbecue cook-offs. With pizza, I remember I was subscribing to pizza magazines all the way back in 1993 when I got married. That was 20 years before I owned a pizza restaurant, so it's been something I've been passionate about for a long time.

Madison

I actually went from wanting to be a teacher to being a sign language interpreter and then to all these different things. Every summer I'd come back here and work to pay for college, and every year this job was more and more fun. It's hard work. Long hours, long days, especially in the busy season, but it's the most rewarding job I've ever had.

Roots

Which style do you prefer? The pizza here or your pizza at Cafe Myth?

Bob

You know, it depends on when you ask me. When I'm down here a few days, I end up craving the pizza up at Benson. When I'm up there, it's the reverse.

Roots

What did you do before you owned Local Myth?

Bob

I was in global supply chain management. So, take your iPhone, right? Who makes it? Apple? Actually not. Apple designs it, develops and engineers it and markets it. But it's actually made by a company in China. Apple subcontracts the actual manufacturing to someone else. And that process can get pretty complex.

For example, you can't just make an iPhone and ship it to Brazil and start selling it.

Every country has different restrictions and requirements. In Brazil, the camera lens must be made from a place called Manaus. It's the law for selling any kind of camera.

The company I worked for, we worked with major tech companies like GoPro, Microsoft, AT&T, and we helped them get their products manufactured, shipped and sold around the world.

Caden
I think I've been working here since I was 10. I just graduated college. I'll be going to law school next.

Madison
I had actually gone to school to be a sign language interpreter. I got the degree, and then right when I got out I was diagnosed with tendonitis. So here I've got this degree and a job, but I can't really do the job because of my tendonitis. You can't do all that signing if you've got wrist issues, right?

Then Bob says to me: you should go back and get your business degree. Then come back and we'll put you to work here managing.

Roots
What do you like most about owning a restaurant?

Bob
Being the boss! Actually, I'm mostly kidding about that. I feel like I'm not really the boss. I feel like I work for the whole team and help them to make their jobs better. I get to do a little bit of everything: make pizzas, make dough, go shopping, whatever. Last night I was here installing a new dishwasher.

Owning a business, especially a restaurant, you have to be a jack of all trades. You need to be a good business person, be a good mechanic, be a decent plumber, an okay electrician. There's just so much that has to be done, and you can't call the plumber every time your sink leaks.

Madison
It's too expensive.

Bob
Right. You have to learn to fix most things yourself.

Madison
I think, too, we just work with the greatest people. Our team, we're all friends. We consider ourselves like family. There's not much we wouldn't do for each other. Anything we need, I think we all feel like we can ask each other for anything, and

that's the whole staff, not just us. It's a great feeling working with people like that.

Caden

That's really true. I had to write an essay before graduation about what place you consider home. And I've moved around a lot. I've lived in Texas, up here, other places for college. But I wrote about Local Myth. When I come to work, it's like walking into my living room. In fact, I prefer to be here than to be at home. There's more food here!

Roots

What's a typical day look like for you?

Bob

One of the perks of owning a pizza restaurant is you don't have to be a morning person. We don't start the day until about 11 or so.

Roots

Your staff looks very young.

Madison

They are. We like to hire kids in high school. That's our mindset. We like to give kids their first jobs. We find a lot of hardworking kids, and they stay on for a long time. They often stay through high school and then keep working when they move on to college.

But there's another aspect too. Like every business in Chelan, we're very seasonal. We have to lay off a lot of staff during the winter. So let's say we hire a single mother or something, and then at the end of the summer, we have to let her go until next summer. Now she's out of work, and that's not good. With high school and college, though, those kids go right back into school, and they go with money in their pockets.

Roots

Is it harder to make pizza here or up at Benson?

Bob

It's the same system at both locations, but the menu and ingredients are different. How it's made is different too because we have machines here but up at Benson everything is hand-pressed.

The prepping is much harder here. We have far more ingredients down here. Up at Benson, they have like 20 ingredients, but we have 86 down here.

We always start our training here at Local Myth. Once they've got it down here, we can send them up to Benson. If you can do it here, you can do it up there no problem.

LONE PINE

Lone Pine Fruit Stand

We visited with Jenny Robelia, the manager of Lone Pine, which is located on the Columbia River. In addition to becoming one of the most successful fruit stands in the area, Lone Pine has also become the final resting place of paraphernalia from various Chelan restaurants that have gone out of business, such as the old Dale's Tavern sign and faded menus from Goochi's and Studio C.

Roots

How did you craft your menu?

Jenny

When we first opened, we weren't really sure we were going to do food. We're a little out of the way down here on the river. It's the middle of nowhere, right? We're eight miles outside of Chelan and about 45 miles or so from East Wenatchee. So we started with an assortment of fruit we were harvesting from our orchards. We did espresso. But we realized pretty quick that with espresso people were also going to want something to eat. So we did little pastries, things like that. But we didn't know how the food service was going to work. Should we do sandwiches? Soup? More?

What we did was we went to a sandwich shop in town and bought some sandwiches and put them in our case to see if people would buy them or not. And they did. They sold real well. So from there we thought: well, let's do sandwiches and go from there.

Roots

What did you do before managing Lone Pine?

Jenny

I was born and raised in Chelan. I worked in different places around town every summer. I worked in restaurants. I worked in a video store. And then this was just a natural fit. Lone Pine combined a lot of my experience and the things I really loved, like agriculture and food, and I've just stayed with it here all these years.

Roots

Did you always want to work in the restaurant industry?

Jenny

No. I thought I'd probably be a teacher or go into a field where I got to work with kids. And I had various experiences in those fields, which I enjoyed.

Roots

What do you like most about running a restaurant and fruit stand?

Jenny

I love seeing so many people. We really offer a space that brings people together, people get to visit and spend time with each other over a sandwich or a slice of pie. That's my favorite thing: to see people with their grandkids or folks that have been friends for 50 years, they come and sit together and have a meal. It's very rewarding.

Roots
What does a normal day look like for you?

Jenny
A normal day starts around 6:00 in the morning. Some days are ordering days. There's always a lot of prep work where you're facilitating your staff and making sure they have what they need to do their jobs. Then there's waiting on customers, answering phones, cleaning, stocking, a little bit of everything. I love being busy, so it's really non-stop until 5:00. Then we lock up, but we're still here until 7:00 or 8:00.

Roots
What did you find most surprising about running a restaurant?

Jenny
Great question. I was most surprised by how when you're this far away from the core of Chelan, how far people will travel to come to see you. With us, or with a restaurant like Blueberry Hills, you see that. People go a long way, and we're always seeing new people every day. Every day we have an opportunity to make a first impression.

Roots
Are most of your customers just passing through?

Jenny
In the summer we obviously get a lot of tourists coming down from Chelan. But through the majority of the year, we get lots of travelers, folks coming off the road who want to take a break and relax, get some food. They're fast travelers.

And we cater to a lot of construction workers and pickers, people who are just on a break for lunch. They have a limited amount of time. That's part of the reason we have a more limited menu. Many of our customers don't have time to sit and wait a long time. They've got just enough time for a sandwich or soup, pastries or pies.

Roots
How did you guys get through COVID?

Jenny
That was hard. We had to make a lot of shifts and adjustments to make things work. What we learned through that time was people really didn't want things to change. They wanted us to be able to return to what we'd been doing before the pandemic, and to be able to do it the way we had been before everything got shut down.

Roots

How long have you had the koi fish out in your pond?

Jenny

Three of them, I call them the OGs because they're from the very first fish we put in the pond 20 years ago. There are nine of them out there total right now. The whole pond froze over this winter, but they all made it. They do amazing.

Roots

You source your own produce locally, is that right?

Jenny

Yes. We grow our own apples, peaches, cherries, some nectarines and apricots and plums. All of those are grown right here in our orchards. We have acreage on this side of the road and across the highway as well. Our blueberries we get from growers in Manson, and we work with growers in Quincy as well. We get a lot of corn out of Quincy. We have a farmer in Pasco that we get asparagus from.

Roots

How old is this building? Was it always a fruit stand?

Jenny

This building was originally an apple packing shed. They packed apples here from about 1900 to the 1930s or 1940s. There's still writing on the walls from where they were counting apples as they packed, counting boxes. Then it changed into picking cabins. They actually put up dividers here and turned it into five cabins. You can see the painted ceiling. Each cabin would have had a living area, bathroom, kitchen, bedroom, all in one square. Very tiny. It stayed that way until 1998. That's when it became the fruit stand.

Roots

That must have required a lot of renovation.

Jenny

It did. The building is very old. Everything inside had to be pulled out and then they had to rethink the entire use of the space. But much of the building is original. The floors are the same floors they built in 1900. This is the same old wood. Same ceiling. The building has great bones.

But they had to work around some of the old construction. The lights for example. You see how the lights are not recessed into the ceiling? That's because above the ceiling is three feet of sawdust. That's what they used for insulation a hundred years ago.

Roots

What are these wood squares on the ceiling?

Jenny

So when they were renovating years ago, they're hammering and moving things around, and the knot holes in the wood would fall out. And then the sawdust would start streaming out of the ceiling onto the floor. So the builders cut a bunch of squares and covered the holes to stop the sawdust from leaking through.

My favorite part though is that the building and the main house behind it were originally in the riverbed. They had to be moved here after they built the dams. The water level rose, so they had to move the building to higher ground.

Roots

How do you decide what items to stock and sell?

Jenny

Mostly it's people come in and they say: hey, I make this soap, would you be interested in selling it? And you choose things you think people will buy and enjoy. It's all locally made stuff. It's a great way to meet people and learn their story. Where they came from, how they got into making soap or whatever, how they make it. Sometimes we go to a show and find a product, or we skim through a catalogue and order something. But most of it is local and we work directly with the person who makes it.

Roots

You host events here in the summer, is that right?

Jenny

Over the years we've done a lot of things. We did a summer concert series. We've done wine tasting. Car shows. Flea markets. Vendor markets. We've done food trucks. Just about everything. It's a great space with a big parking lot that accommodates a lot of people, so over the years we've done a lot of different things.

Roots

We've heard that you have some old memorabilia here on site.

Jenny

We do. We have the Dale's Tavern sign out back. And we have some of the tables they had inside. The one on our porch over there is from Dale's, the one with everyone's name carved into it. I have a sandwich board from Flying Saucers. Lots of old menus from places like Goochi's, which is where The Landing is now. They're fun to look through. You can see how the prices changed over time. You forget how many businesses have come and gone.

It's history. Little bits of history, like the tables. All those people who carved their names. They weren't famous or anything, but it's still a part of the town. You try to hang onto some of that.

MARCELA'S

Marcela's

Marcela Anaya and her husband, Angel Cisneros, opened Marcela's in 2010. Marcela's father had owned a restaurant in downtown Chelan: La Laguna. However, when her father was stricken with cancer, he was forced to close the restaurant. Opening Marcela's was a way of continuing with her father's business. I met with Marcela to discuss her life in the restaurant industry and what she enjoys about running a business here in the Chelan Valley.

Kendall:

In what year did you open your restaurant?

Marcela:

My husband and I opened the restaurant in 2010. So it's been 14 years now.

Kendall:

And you opened the restaurant yourself?

Marcela:

Yes. My father had owned a restaurant here in Chelan called La Laguna. But we opened Marcela's ourselves.

Kendall:

Why did you open Marcelas?

Marcela:

I grew up in the restaurant industry. Like I said, my father owned a restaurant. I worked there when I was just a kid. I refilled the salt and pepper shakers, cleaned the windows, things like that. I loved it. And when I was in high school I worked in my mom's restaurant in Seattle. When my dad came down with cancer, he had to close La Laguna. Opening Marcela's was a way of continuing with the work he'd started.

Kendall:

What do you like best about owning a restaurant?

Marcela:

It's a very rewarding industry. You get to meet so many people, and often you get customers who come in year after year. So you get to connect with these families, see their kids grow up, be a small part of their lives. Running a restaurant is hard. It's a lot of work. But it's very rewarding.

Kendall:

Did you always want to own a restaurant?

Marcela:

No, I wanted to go to school for fashion! That was my original goal. But restaurant work was always in the back of my mind. Both my parents owned restaurants, so it was something I knew a lot about.

Kendall:

What does a normal day look like for you?

Marcela:

My days usually start with paperwork at home. Then I come to the restaurant and see how things are going. I check our inventory, see how our stock is doing. Depending on how busy we are, I may be here all day or I may be able to go home early.

Kendall:

How many employees do you have?

Marcela:

In the off season we get as low as 12, but in the summer it's closer to 30. Summers are very busy.

Kendall:

What were you most surprised about when you opened your restaurant?

Marcela:

At first, I think the most surprising thing was how difficult it was to figure out staffing. Managing people is never easy, and when you've got a decent sized restaurant you have a lot of people to work with, a lot of different schedules. No matter how long you do it, managing people is a challenge.

Kendall:

What kind of food do you serve?

Marcela:

Mexican food with a few exceptions, like chicken strips.

Kendall:

How did you come up with your menu?

Marcela:

Both my mom and dad ran Mexican restaurants. So I had a lot of experience with that. With Marcela's, we wanted a clean kind of Mexican food, something more unique than what you'd usually get in a Mexican restaurant around here. We used a lot of my mom's recipes, but we add items to the menu every six months or so. It's good to change things up from time to time and see how they do.

Kendall:

What is your favorite item on the menu? What is your favorite food in general?

Marcela:

If I had to pick one, it would probably be the pollo al carbon, which is chicken with a chipotle sauce. And I love Asian food. I make it all the time at home.

Kendall:

What is the hardest thing to cook?

Marcela:

Shredded beef. It's not hard to cook, but it's slow cooking and very time consuming.

Kendall:

Where are you from originally?

Marcela:

My parents were both born in Mexico, but I was born and raised in Seattle.

Kendall:

What did you do before you owned a restaurant?

Marcela:

I worked in retail. I worked in a coffee shop. I was a bartender.

Kendall:

What is the newest item on the menu?

Marcela:

It's called Angel's Special. It's rice, onions, peppers and meat with chipotle sauce.

Kendall:

Why should people go to your restaurant?

Marcela:

I'd say we have good clean food, a great staff, excellent customer service. There are other Mexican restaurants in Chelan, but we try to offer our own unique spin on things. I think even if you're used to going to Mexican restaurants, you'll find something to love at Marcela's that you can't get anywhere else.

Kendall:

Is there anything else you want to add?

Marcela:

If you're interested in the restaurant industry, you should go for it. It's a very fun and social job to have.

BIGFOOT
PARKING
ONLY

WOODY'S

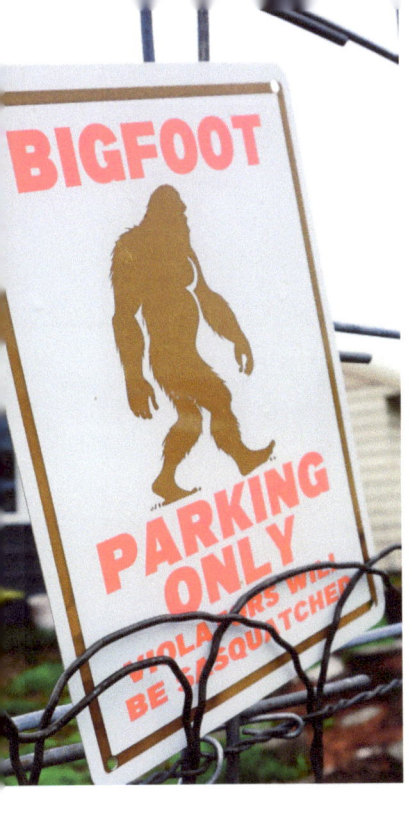

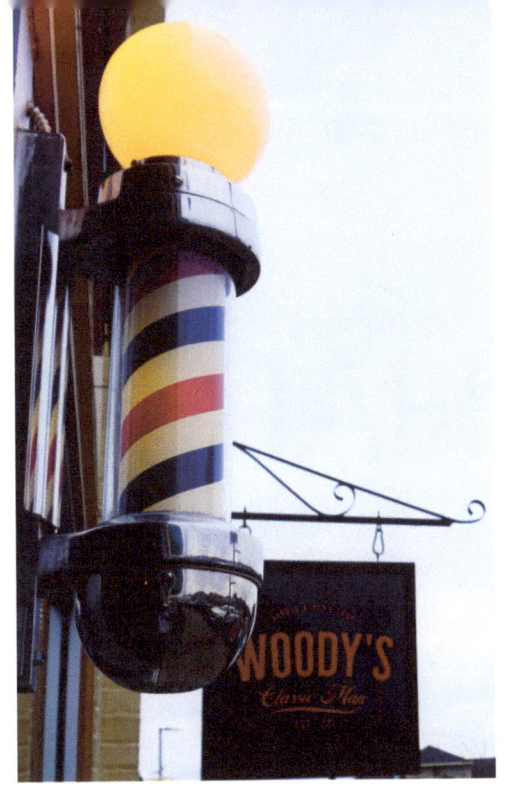

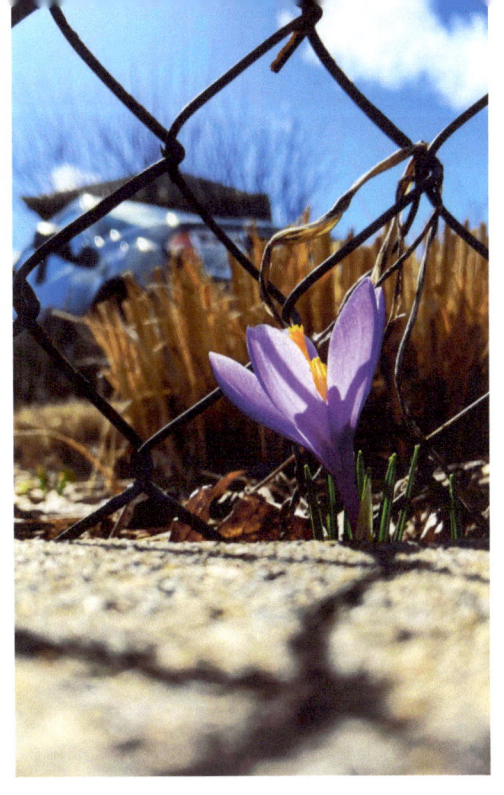

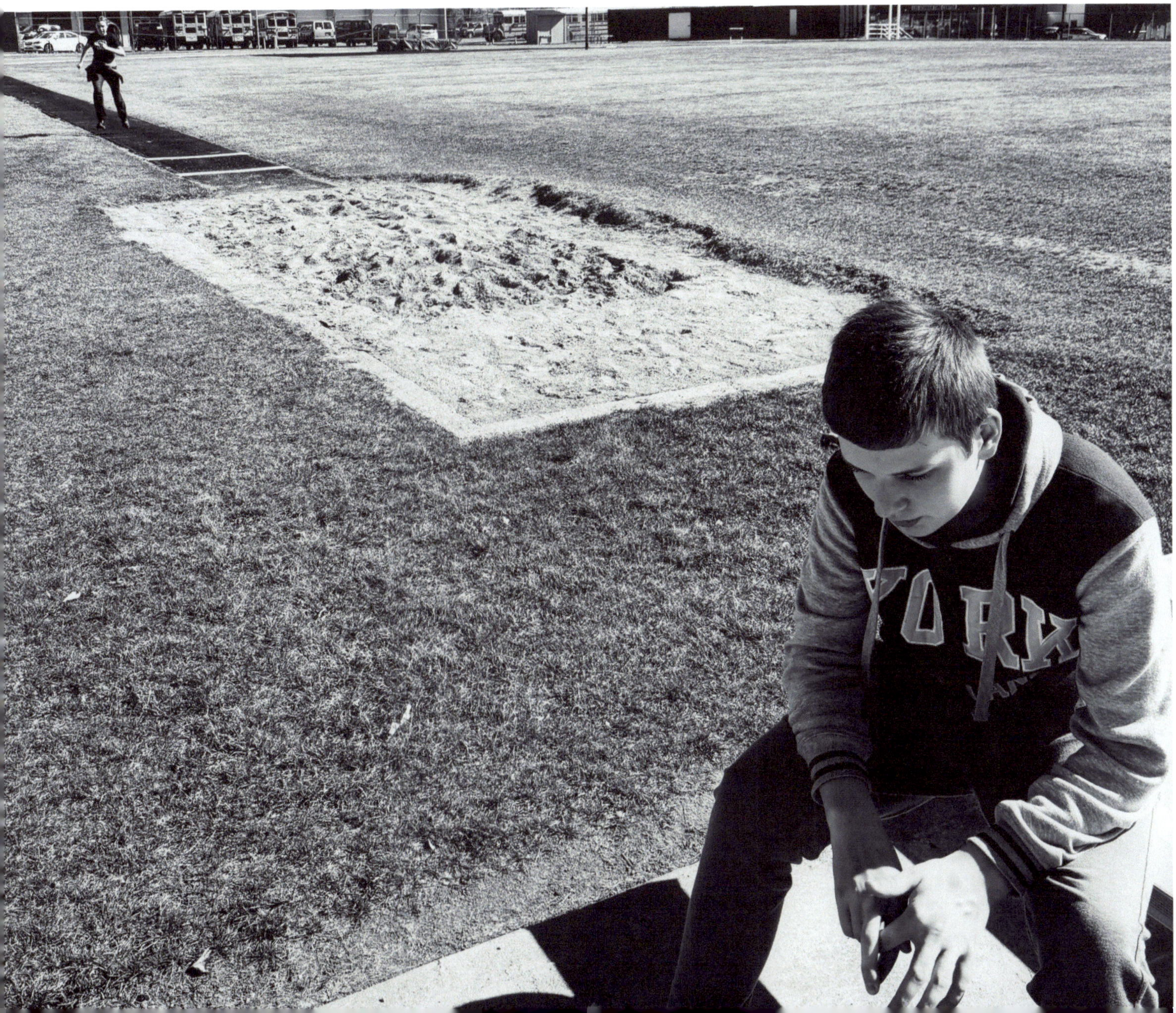
YORK

ORCHARD CAFE

Orchard Cafe

Many people don't realize there's a cafe in the Lake Chelan Hospital at all. Or if they imagine there is one, it doesn't occur to them that anyone -- patient or not -- can stop in and order food. And not the kind of bland and unappealing food hospitals are typically known for, but rather high-quality food made by a trained chef.

I sat down with Chef Tyler Ehlert to discuss his background in the culinary arts, as well as what he enjoys about being a chef in a place where most people don't think they'll ever find top notch food.

Isabell
Did you always want to be a chef?

Tyler
No. I went to college for an English major because I wanted to be a teacher. Two years in, though, I just wasn't enjoying it. But I'd always loved to cook. My mom's a chef and I started cooking in the summer and it just carried over. I ended up at culinary school in Vancouver. That was 32 years ago.

Isabell
What do you enjoy cooking for yourself?

Tyler
Tough question. I love so many styles of food. Probably Asian. Japanese and Thai are favorites. I love making sushi.

Isabell
A lot of the chef's we've talked to really enjoy making sushi.

Tyler
It takes a specific skill set, and you've gotta be very patient. But it's a lot of fun.

Isabell
What do you like most about working here?

Tyler
I love cooking for the patients. When a patient isn't feeling well, I like making them something that's healthy and will make them happy. I like to think I've helped them improve on their condition just a bit. Being at a hospital can be stressful, so it's nice for there to be a space where people can eat really quality food. Hospital food doesn't have the best reputation. It's nice that people can come in and know they're getting a great meal.

Isabell

Where are you from originally?

Tyler

All over. I'm Canadian. Grew up in Southern Alberta. I moved to the States when I was 19. Started college and university and been here ever since.

Isabell

When did you become the chef here at the cafe?

Tyler

I started here five years ago, but I left for a year and went to the hospital in Wenatchee, then came back here. I've worked kitchens in hospitals since 2000.

Isabell

You worked at the old hospital here in Chelan? Our school, Roots, is located there.

Tyler

Yep. I was there.

Isabell

What draws you to working in a hospital cafe?

Tyler

I've got four kids. Three still in school. Chefs working in restaurants tend to work late. You work a lot of holidays and weekends. Here at the hospital, I don't have to do that. I work Monday through Friday. I'm home by dinner. No weekends and most holidays off. For a chef, that's pretty rare.

Isabell

What's your official role?

Tyler

Director of Environmental Dietary Services. I create the menus, hire the staff, train them, keep everything running. I've got a great crew here.

Isabell

How do you like this new location for the hospital?

Tyler

Well it's a brand new building. Love that. It's got great big windows with a lot of sun shining in. We've got this beautiful new kitchen where people can watch us preparing fresh food. I actually got to design this kitchen the way I wanted to. It was great to spec out all the equipment and layout. It's like getting all the toys you wanted at Christmas and now I get to play with them every day.

Isabell

In what ways did your design improve over the old hospital?

Tyler

It's more simplified now. Everything's in a straight logical line from prep to serving. And you can see everything as the customer. Sometimes I get creeped out not knowing where my food comes from if I'm in a restaurant. What's going on in the kitchen, right? Are they wearing gloves? Washing their hands? Here, people can clearly see what's going on and what choices we're making. And even though we're small, we can actually serve 500 people if necessary.

Isabell

What kind of food do you serve?

Tyler

It's a six-week rotating menu based on what's fresh and in season. When the weather warms up, I'll start lightening up the entrees, do more salads. In the winter, we do more soups and stews, burritos and pasta. Our patients get special treatment. We have a Patient Ambassador program, and our Ambassadors check in on the patients to see specifically what they need food wise, or maybe they have family with them and their family would like a meal.

Isabell

Do you source your food locally?

Tyler

Absolutely. For example, we buy from Anderson Farms. They have gorgeous blueberries we use for the season and freeze for the rest of the year. As a hospital, we have to be very careful about where we get our food.

Honestly, I end up doing a lot of research. We've got our vendors, and I have to look at what's fresh, what's in season, and base the menus off that. And then I have to talk to staff, see if people are eating what we're making and enjoying the meals. If not, then it's time to switch things up.

Isabell

What do items cost on the menu?

Tyler

Entrees range from $5 to $7. They're priced depending on the price of ingredients. I usually stay away from expensive stuff like King Crab. I mean, our patients might love it if crab were on the menu, but it's not exactly within our price point.

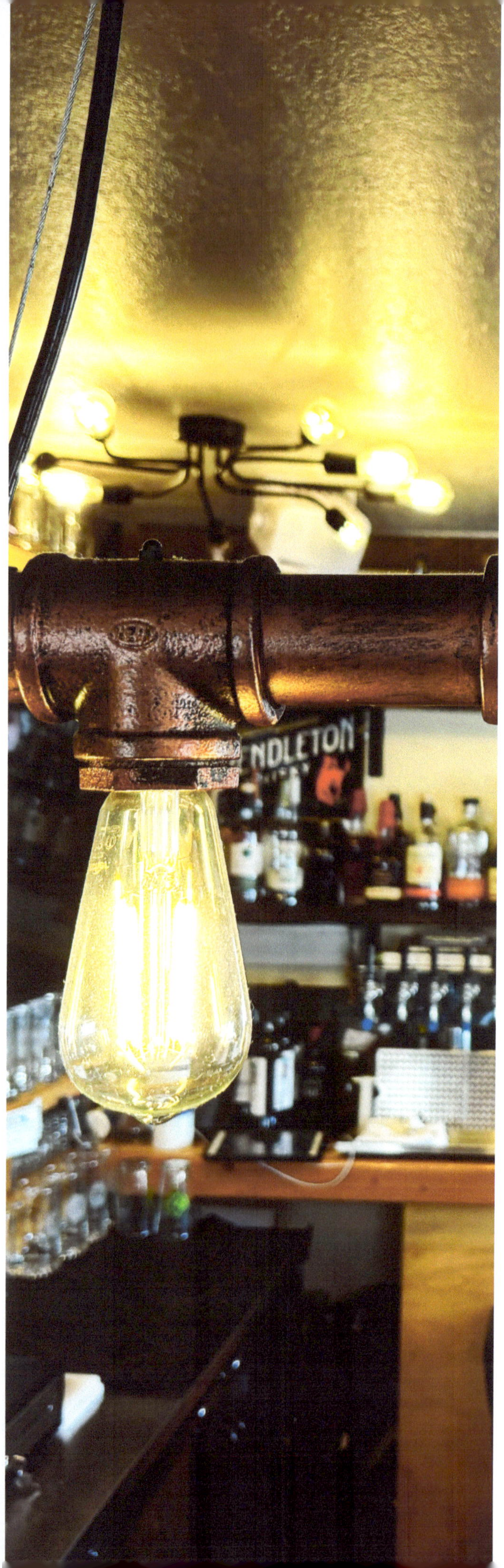
ENDLETON

STOP

Chelan
BRARY
PEN!
SON

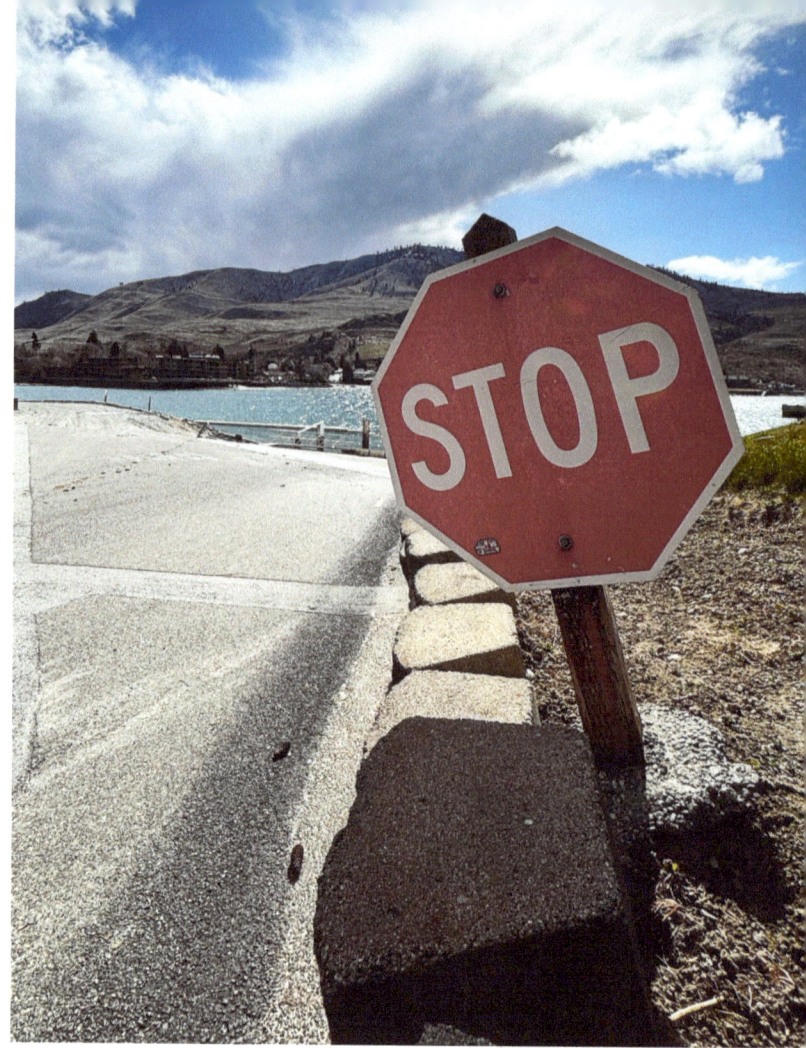

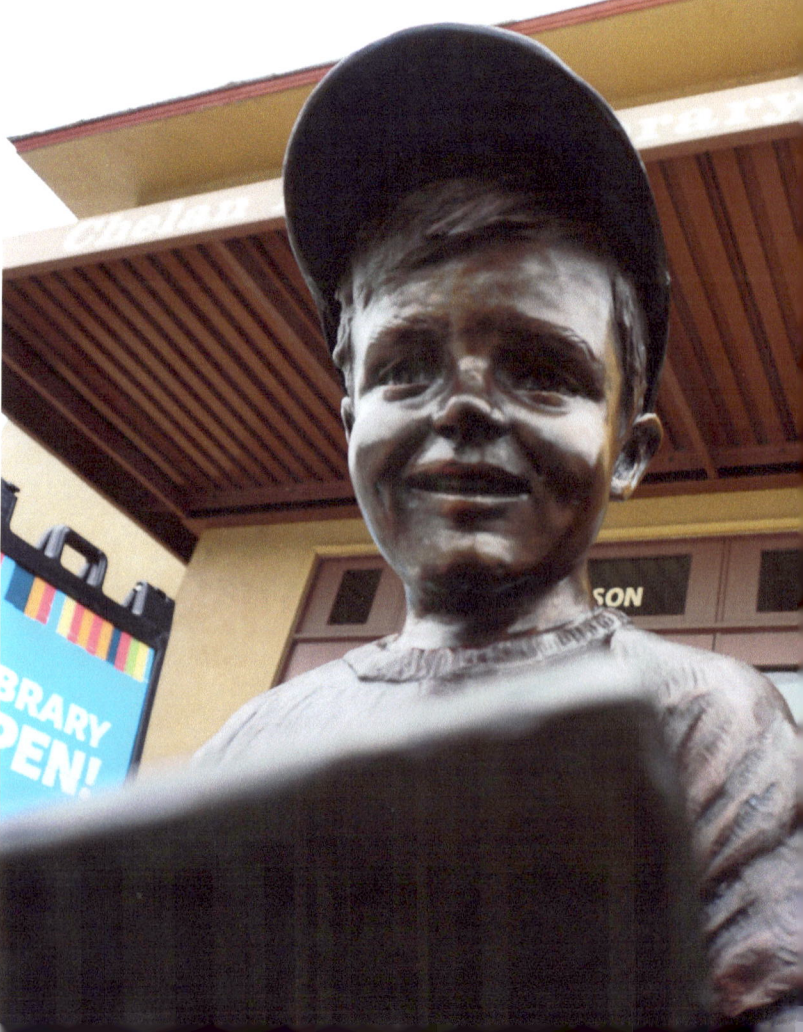

SIREN SONG

Siren Song Winery

Holly Brown and her husband, Kevin, opened Siren Song in 2015. Their goal was to create a Provencal style restaurant and winery experience, one that paired wine inspired by France, Italy and Spain with food created in the European tradition. Holly is both the co-owner and Executive Chef. In addition to overseeing the restaurant operation, she also teaches culinary classes and hosts European wine tours.

In Greek mythology, a siren was a type of mermaid that sang alluring songs to Greek sailors. Over time, the term siren song came to be associated with irresistible attractions and life callings. Siren Song Winery hopes to offer just such an attraction: a fantastic place to enjoy wonderful wine and great food. Holly was out of the country when I contacted her about an interview. However, she was willing to correspond by email.

Grant:
You opened Siren Song in 2015, correct?

Siren Song:
Yes, the winery opened in 2015, but we had been making wine since 2007.

Grant:
How many employees do you have?

Siren Song:
Our team size changes pretty dramatically seasonally with about 15 employees year-round to about 30 in the summertime.

Grant:
What kind of food do you serve?

Siren Song:
Our menu is inspired by European cuisine including French, Italian, and Spanish style food and wine pairings.

Grant:
How did you start Siren Song?

Siren Song:
We initially bought the 7 acre vineyard that Siren Song now sits on and we designed and built the building and business from scratch. My husband and I are the owners. My husband Kevin is the winemaker and I am the executive chef.

Grant:
Why did you choose to open a winery?

Siren Song:
We love France and Europe, and we wanted to re-create an experience that reminded us of Bistro life which is very typical in Europe where you hang out, have a glass of wine and some food and relax and watch the world go by.

The name Siren Song comes from Greek mythology. A Siren Song is an irresistible attraction, it inspires one to think about what they are meant to be or do.

Grant:
What did you do before you owned Siren Song?

Siren Song:
We have been entrepreneurs. We owned and invested in multiple companies and business types. Kevin had a finance and tech background before he studied to be a winemaker. I was in marketing and media before I went to culinary school.

Grant:
Why did you decide to serve the particular type of food you serve?

Siren Song:
As a winery, we wanted our food to complement and pair well with our wine. And we wanted to create a typical French bistro experience.

Grant:
Where are you from originally?

Siren Song:
California.

Grant:
What do you like most about owning a winery?

Siren Song:
Meeting people. Creating a beautiful food and wine experience for our guests.

Grant:
What does a normal day look like for you?

Siren Song:
Very busy! From overseeing the day to day operation, menu planning, marketing, creating events, and working on new business concepts, including additional locations.

Grant:
What were you most surprised by once you opened your winery?

Siren Song:
The seasonality of business.

Grant:
How did you create your menu?

Siren Song:
The menu is inspired by my travel experiences, seasonal ingredients and flavor profiles that I think people will enjoy, but will also be unique and that pair with wine. Beauty on the plate is also important because we eat with our eyes. Fresh uncomplicated food is always the best!

Grant:
What is the hardest thing to cook on your menu?

Siren Song:
Pizza requires skill and heart. All cooking requires talent, but some things require experience and nuance. Our Neapolitan style pizza is made from scratch in-house, including our dough and sauce. To make and work with dough takes time to learn.

Grant:
What do you like about running a winery in Chelan?

Siren Song:
Chelan is a beautiful place where we love being part of the community.

Grant:
Did you always want to own a winery?

Siren Song:
Nope. Never imagined.

Grant:
Why should people go to your winery?

Siren Song:
It's a beautiful place with wonderful hospitality, yummy food, and not only award-winning wine, but truly delicious wine made with great love!

VIN DU LAC

Vin Du Lac Winery

I visited with Larry Lehmbecker, owner of Vin Du Lac Winery in the early spring. We sat on a bluff overlooking the North Shore of Lake Chelan, which happens to be Vin Du Lac's patio. As we admired the view, I asked Larry why he had opened a winery, especially given that he had been a lawyer before going into the wine business (in fact, he is still a lawyer even now).

We talked about the differences between law and wine, how he had come to craft the menu at Vin Du Lac, and how he was inspired by West Coast wineries in Napa Valley.

JJ:
When did you open the winery?

Vin Du Lac:
We opened for business in 2002. For the first five or six years, we only had deli food. We made baguette sandwiches, things like that. Later we started doing things like paninis. The actual full service restaurant has been open for about 14 years. I think we started that sometime in 2010.

JJ:
How many employees do you have?

Vin Du Lac:
During the wintertime, the restaurant portion of the business typically has six or seven employees. In the summertime that can double. We add kitchen staff and servers and all that. It takes a lot more people.

JJ:
How would you describe your menu?

Vin Du Lac:
I think of our food as fresh Northwest cuisine with French influences. What I mean by that is that we always have fresh produce that we grow here. Any seafood we do we bring in fresh. We focus on foods that are native to the Northwest, salmon and halibut and things that are harvested here.

We also try to use locally raised beef and as much of the local produce as we can. The French influence comes from certain types of dishes and preparations. Our recipes are generally traditional to French classic cooking.

JJ:
Tell us why you started running a restaurant.

Vin Du Lac:

My original inspiration was just to have a winery. I was inspired by wineries I'd seen on the West Coast, particularly in Napa Valley. They had restaurants or fancy delis so you could buy food along with the wine. Obviously food and wine go well together. You like to drink wine with a nice meal, that kind of thing. So it was natural to offer food here as part of the winery experience.

JJ:

What did you do before you owned a restaurant?

Vin Du Lac:

I was a lawyer. In fact, I'm still a lawyer. I have a law practice in Bellevue.

JJ:

How did you craft your menu?

Vin Du Lac:

First, I'd say it's the kind of food I like to eat when I go out. And second, I don't really feel like there are very many other restaurants in North Central Washington that are offering the type of items and the quality of items that we are trying to offer. And so I thought we would be unique by offering this type of menu.

I love eating out at fine restaurants. So there are a lot of dishes I know I enjoy, particular cuisines and such. When I hire a chef, I sit down with them and let them know the cuisines and types of dishes I'm looking for. But the chef's actually have a lot of freedom to create dishes within those cuisines. We have classics like a Caesar salad, right? But then the chef can do something like a kale Caesar, which gives them options to be creative. They can keep it interesting and offer our guests something new.

JJ:

What is your favorite item on the menu?

Vin Du Lac:

That's tricky since our menu changes all the time. Normally I'd say I love our pasta with red sauce. Right now we have a pasta with Alfredo sauce and fresh peas, which I love. When we have salmon, though, salmon is always going to be my first choice.

JJ:

Where are you from originally?

Vin Du Lac:

I grew up in Renton, on the West Side. I used to come to Chelan for summer vacations. This was my favorite place to come. I always wanted to have a place here. And we finally bought property here in 2002 when we opened the winery.

JJ:
What do you like most about owning a restaurant?

Vin Du Lac:
I like that it makes people happy to come here and have a great meal. You can sit on the patio with the view and spend time with your friends and family. It's rewarding knowing that I can provide that experience for people.

JJ:
What does a normal day look like for you?

Vin Du Lac:
Well, for me, I'm more the business manager. I'm not involved in the actual preparation or serving of the food. My restaurant activities typically involve talking to my chef and manager and the servers to make sure all the planning is done. Then it's my job to keep track of all the finances.

Are we making money? Are we losing money? What might need fixing?

JJ:
What were you most surprised about when you opened your restaurant?

Vin Du Lac:
How hard it is to make money in this business. It's very difficult. It's easy for costs to get out of control. And the seasonality of it is tough. We do three to four times the amount of business in the summer than we do in the winter. So winters are hard to generate enough business to pay for the staff.

JJ:
What is your role role in the restaurant?

Vin Du Lac:
Specifically, I'm the Senior Manager. I have a General Manager who has a lot of authority, but ultimately choices about setting the budget, is the menu meeting our standards, are staff providing quality service and food, those things are up to me. Those are my decisions.

If I don't think we're going a good enough job, then I step in and provide direction to get things back on track. But that's more of an oversight thing. It's not really a daily task sort of role. That's what my General Manager does.

JJ:
What do you like about running a restaurant in Chelan?

Vin Du Lac:
I love that we're able to serve outside much of the year. That people can sit and eat

outside. I think dining outside has a special charm to it. So here in Chelan, that's a real advantage. People can come and sit outside and have a great meal and enjoy the view.

JJ:
Did you always want to own a restaurant?

Vin Du Lac:
Probably since I was a teenager, I thought it would be very cool to have a restaurant. It's been a dream of mine for a long time. Also owning a winery, although I wasn't thinking about that as a teenager. The restaurant idea definitely came first.

My parents used to take us out quite a bit as kids, and we learned to enjoy going out to eat as a family. I just always thought it would be cool to have a place and give other families that same experience.

JJ:
Why should people come to Vin Du Lac?

Vin Du Lac:
If you want really fresh food from a chef that really specializes in high-quality Northwest and French cuisine, you should check us out. We're probably the only place around that you can really find that. Don't get me wrong. There are great restaurants here, but I think we really try to be the best in terms of the freshest products, the most interesting dishes, and then it's just a beautiful place to eat.

I mean look around here. This view. What more could you ask for?

THE VOGUE

The Vogue Coffee Bar

We met with Zack Dickson who, along with his wife Mary, own The Vogue Coffee Bar in downtown Chelan. The Vogue has been a mainstay for our team, a place we visit every week to enjoy coffee, relax, write and read. We have held many classes at The Vogue throughout the year. No matter the weather – rain, wind, snow – our team has made the trip week after week. It was a real pleasure to sit down with Zack to learn more about the inner workings of running a coffee shop.

Roots

Tell us about how you came to own The Vogue.

Zack

So my wife and I, we're the second owners. The original owner, Mike Cooney, opened it in 2005. Mike was mayor of Chelan a few years back. He sold it to us in 2021, right in the middle of the COVID pandemic.

Roots

Were you concerned about buying a business during a pandemic?

Zack

A lot of people questioned our decision. Was that the best time to buy? Would it be better to wait? But we recognized how popular the Vogue was, that it's become a kind of institution and that people love going there. We had faith the pandemic would pass and the Vogue would still be a popular place to come and hang out. And we were right, I think. We did some revitalizing of the interior, and we've been really lucky to see our popularity not be significantly impacted.

Roots

What kind of food do you focus on?

Zack

What we do is called quick service. We prep food in the back and have a refrigerated case up front. We have food that we can heat up quickly or items that don't require cooking, like salads or yogurt cups. Our high speed oven can cook sandwiches really fast, so we do breakfast sandwiches and lunch sandwiches. Frittatas, quiches, those kinds of things. We try to stock a variety. We have four kinds of lunch sandwiches, for example, and three different salads. That way people have some options.

Roots

Did you always want to own a restaurant?

Zack

My wife and I were interested in owning our own business. Neither of us knew much about coffee, to be honest, but we'd worked in hospitality and in food service. When the opportunity came up to buy The Vogue, it just seemed like the perfect idea. Mike wanted to sell it to someone who wanted to carry on the coffee shop and keep the Vogue as a local gathering place. That was attractive to us.

Roots
What did you do before owning The Vogue?

Zack
I worked in a number of places around town. I worked at Campbell's and a bunch of the wineries. I worked for Chase Bank for a while as a teller and in home loans.

Roots
How did you build out your menu?

Zack
We knew from the start what we wanted to do was be able to make quality products quickly. People are in a hurry, they're grabbing a coffee and out they go. So we knew that had to be the cornerstone: quality and speed. But we wanted to also put a little spin on things to make them more distinct. For example, we add a homemade garlic aioli onto our ham and egg breakfast sandwich. It makes that sandwich standout from what someone like Starbucks is doing.

Roots
Did you grow up around here?

Zack
No. I grew up in Southern California in Laguna Beach, about halfway between LA and San Diego. I moved to Chelan in 2016. My wife, Mary, she's from the West Side. We wanted to be closer to her family, and we'd always enjoyed the small town community. We visited here a number of times and just really loved the people, loved the community, loved the lake of course. Chelan has a real special vibe. With the lake and the agriculture and the people, it's just very different from everywhere else.

Roots
What's a normal day look like for you?

Zack
It's all over the place right now. I have a three and a half month baby girl, which just changes things up a lot. Usually though I'd be at The Vogue around 6:00. I'll spend a lot of time in the kitchen prepping, and I'll work to about 12:00 or 1:00. Our baristas come around 6:30. We close up around 4:00 and clean for an hour or so.

Roots
What were you most surprised by when you bought the restaurant?

Zack

There are a lot of surprises! I don't think I anticipated how much maintenance goes into keeping the place running well. All the equipment that needs maintenance. We have so many different refrigerators, and we've got blenders and espresso machines, all kinds of stuff. And you have to learn how to take care of all those machines, that way you can save some money and keep your doors open.

Roots

Did you make any significant changes to the menu when you bought the restaurant?

Zack

We based the menu on what Mike had done, but we tried to elevate it and make it even better. We were inspired by how he had set up the quick service, but we went through every item and tried to imagine ways to upgrade the ingredients and make things just that much more interesting and tasty and memorable.

I have friends who've owned places here in town or who have been chefs in different restaurants in Chelan, and they gave me a lot of assistance in updating the menu and understanding what we could accomplish.

Roots

What's the most challenging item on the menu to make?

Zack

We have a veggie bon mi. It's not necessarily hard, but you have to pickle three different kinds of vegetables, so it takes more time than the other sandwiches.

Roots

What do you like most about owning The Vogue?

Zack

The community, for sure. Interacting with the community. And being a place where people can come in and work and meet with friends and family. I really enjoy providing a space for that.

Roots

Did you always see yourself as someone who would one day own a restaurant?

Zack

No, I'd never really considered it. I knew I wanted to be my own boss, and I was interested in food. I used to have a small market garden. I grew vegetables for the farmer's market, a weekly vegetable subscription people could come and pick up. I enjoyed cooking. But those things had never really come together in my mind like: yes, I want to own a restaurant. It's been a big learning curve. Just learning how to make coffee has been a learning curve.

Roots

What was the biggest challenge you faced in taking over the restaurant from the previous owner?

Zack

The Vogue was really popular already, and people knew Mike really well. So just trying to fill those shoes. But the community was, I'd say, really stoked to have someone carrying on the business and not trying to turn it into something totally different. We had a great outpouring of support right from the start.

We made changes to the layout and the interior, and you know when you change things there's always a certain amount of pushback. But overall everyone has been very supportive and encouraging.

Roots

How many pounds of coffee do you go through in a week?

Zack

We get our coffee from Blue Star in Twisp. It comes in five-pound bags. In the summer I'd say we go through 120 pounds a week. That's espresso, drip, all of it.

Roots

What's the hardest drink to make?

Zack

We have a special drink called a Sweet Caroline. Two shots espresso, a little vanilla, a bit of steamed milk. Then we do what's called expressing the orange. Then a bit of orange zest and some cinnamon on the rim. It's the most involved drink we make. It's wonderful.

Roots

Did you guys make any updates to the machinery when you bought the place?

Zack

Yeah, like we bought a La Marzocco espresso machine. It was the first one of that model in North America to be installed. The owner of Blue Star Coffee encouraged us to get that, and it makes a big difference in the quality of the espresso. Total game changer.

The Vogue always made good coffee, but we've really tried to up the game. We're always trying to improve, you know?

WHO

IS

LEO

MONTAIGNE?

We Are Leo

Roots Community School

We Are Leo Montaigne

Roots Community School is a private school in Lake Chelan. Our school is made up of five classes across kindergarten to eighth grade. Typically two grades are paired together in a class.

Our seventh/eighth grade class is called the Mountain Lions. To determine a pseudonym for this book, we examined the roots words for both *mountain* and *lion.*

Lion comes from the Old French word *Leo*, while *Mountain* derives from another French word: *Montaigne.*

Thus Leo Montaigne was born.

However, Leo isn't just one person. In fact, he's twelve. Our class is made up of eight boys and four girls. We are:

- Isabell Ahlers
- Kendall Bordner
- Fletcher Brandt
- Grant Cook
- Logan Frahm
- Beau Fricke
- Dean Hinckley
- Tiana Inda
- Wyatt Sather
- JJ Stockdale
- Grace Whitehall
- Ethan Wright

Thank you for reading our cookbook. We hope that you learned something about Lake Chelan and enjoyed the recipes shared with us by these local restaurants and community members.

Sincerely,

The Mountain Lions

Beau & Fletch

Crafting a Local Cookbook

The Lake Chelan Cookbook project came out of our Language Arts & History class. Our goal was to study the culinary history of Lake Chelan and showcase it through this book. To make that happen, we did a considerable amount of writing, much of which was never intended to make it into the book. For example, after speaking with so many employers, we spent weeks writing and refining our own resumes. We also wrote emails to prospective media outlets, and composed reflection pieces on what we had learned throughout this project, and crafted think-pieces on what kinds of photos we wanted to capture during our community photo shoots.

Logan

Getting Just the Right Shot

Photographs are the backbone of a good cookbook, and in our case we wanted to document not just food but the Chelan Valley itself. To that end, we worked with two professional photographers who shared their time and their wisdom: Jen Brandt and Richard Ulhorn. Both provided guidance and insight.

To capture our photos, we used a variety of devices: Canons, Nikons, and a range of cell phones. If you spotted a roving band of young teenagers drifting through town snapping photos of everything and doing their best to look like tourists, that was us. We shot over 6,000 photos to make this book.

Kendall & Wyatt

Touring the Culinary Valley

In order to write about the culinary world here in Chelan, we first had to get out there and experience it ourselves. For months we set up field trips and interviews with local restaurants, wineries and businesses. THANK YOU to all the business owners who put up with us and gave so graciously of their time. Touring restaurants and tasting food was definitely the most enjoyable part of the entire project. All of the restaurants featured in this book either sat down with us for an interview or hosted us for a tour. Many let us into kitchens, warehouses, and facilities not usually shown to the public. We met so many incredibly generous business owners who provided tremendous insight into how the culinary world really works.

Acknowledgements

First and foremost we would like to thank all of the restaurants that hosted us throughout this project, that gave generously of their time, that shared their recipes with us, and that toured us through their facilities. This entire project would not be possible without their generosity and dedication to our community.

Second, a big thank you to all the community members who submitted recipes to this project, who aided us in finding local dishes, and who encouraged and supported this project from the start.

And finally, thank you to our parents who endured our efforts to cook a wide variety of recipes at home. Your support in all that we do, and your dedication to our education, is invaluable. We love you.